CH

D0468550

DISCARD

WESTMINSTER PUBLIC LIBRARY
3705 W. 112TH AVE.
WESTMINSTER, CO 80031

MAY 07

Scrapbooking
Techniques
for Beginners

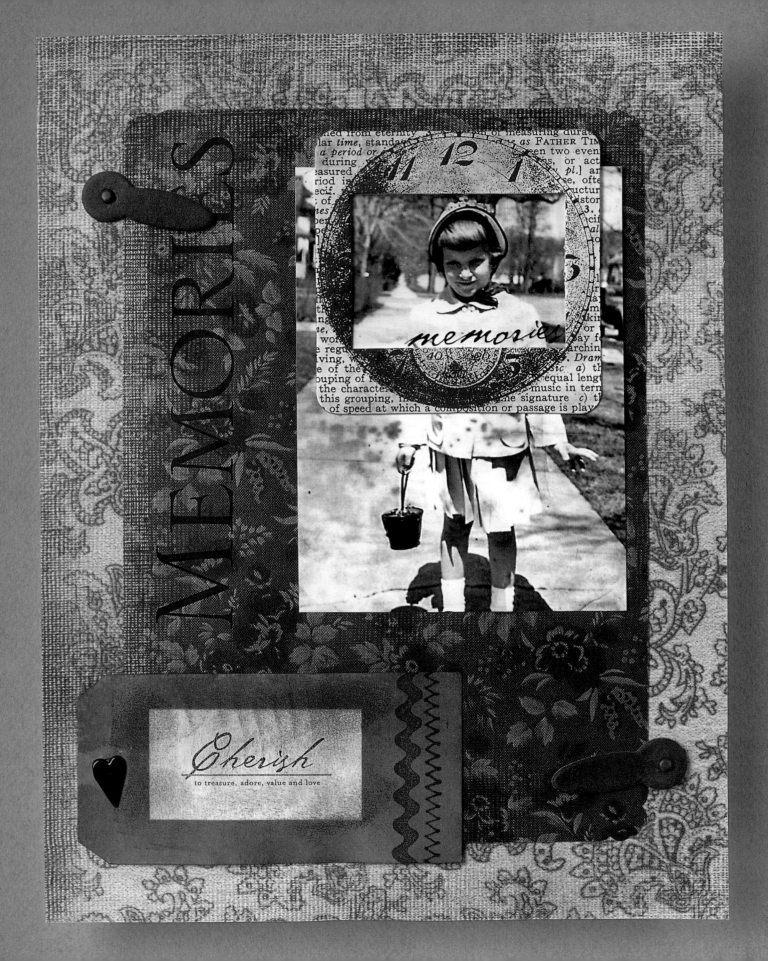

Scrapbooking Techniques for Beginners

Rebekah Meier

Sterling Publishing Co., Inc.
New York

Prolific Impressions Production Staff:
Editor in Chief: Mickey Baskett
Copy Editor: Phyllis Mueller
Graphics: Karen Turpin
Styling: Lenos Key
Photography: Jerry Mucklow
Administration: Jim Baskett

Every effort has been made to insure that the information presented is accurate. Since we have no control over physical conditions, individual skills, or chosen tools and products, the publisher disclaims any liability for injuries, losses, untoward results, or any other damages which may result from the use of the information in this book. Thoroughly read the instructions for all products used to complete the projects in this book, paying particular attention to all cautions and warnings shown for that product to ensure their proper and safe use.

No part of this book may be reproduced for commercial purposes in any form without permission by the copyright holder. The written instructions and design patterns in this book are intended for the personal use of the reader and may be reproduced for that purpose only.

Library of Congress Cataloging-in-Publication Data Available
Meier, Rebekah, 1962-
   Scrapbooking techniques for beginners / Rebekah Meier.
        p. cm.
   Includes index.
   ISBN-13: 978-1-4027-3504-2
   ISBN-10: 1-4027-3504-9
1. Photograph albums. 2. Photographs--Conservation and restoration. 3. Scrapbooks. I. Title.
TR465.M43 2007
745.593--dc22

                                                                            2006029291

2   4   6   8   10   9   7   5   3   1

Published by Sterling Publishing Co., Inc.
387 Park Avenue South, New York, NY 10016
© 2007 by Prolific Impressions, Inc.
Distributed in Canada by Sterling Publishing
c/o Canadian Manda Group, 165 Dufferin Street,
Toronto, Ontario, Canada M6K 3H6
Distributed in the United Kingdom by GMC Distribution Services,
Castle Place, 166 High Street, Lewes, East Sussex, England BN7 1XU
Distributed in Australia by Capricorn Link (Australia) Pty. Ltd.
P.O. Box 704, Windsor, NSW 2756, Australia

Printed in China
All rights reserved

ISBN-13: 978-1-4027-3504-2
ISBN-10: 1-4027-3504-9

For information about custom editions, special sales, premium and
corporate purchases, please contact Sterling Special Sales
Department at 800-805-5489 or specialsales@sterlingpub.com.

About the Author

Rebekah Meier is a self-taught multi media decorative artist and designer. Working within the craft industry 22 years she has made a career of designing products for manufacturers, authoring books and magazine articles, teaching, and demonstrating.

She lives in northern Illinois with her husband of 25 years and their two wonderful boys.

Dedication

To my husband, Brad, and sons, Dan and Matt, whose love and support mean so much to me. To my mother, Helen – your daily help and love keeps me going.

Acknowledgements

Special thanks to the following companies for their generous contributions of supplies for creating the scrapbook pages in this book:

Basic Grey Papers for supplying papers for the book; 1343 Flint Meadow Drive #6, Kaysville, UT 84037, www.basicgrey.com

Bazzill Basics Paper for their wonderful papers; 501 East Comstock Dr., Chandlier, AZ 85225, www.bazzillbasics.com

Fiskars for scissors and other tools; 2537 Daniels St. Madison, WI 53718, www.fiskars.com

Me and My Big Ideas for rub-on transfers, stickers, and embellishments; 20321 Valencia Circle, Lake Forest, CA 92630, www.meandmybigideas.com

Plaid Enterprises, Inc. for Papier Paint, stencils, and stamps; P.O. Box 7600, Norcross, GA 30091-7600, www.plaidonline.com

Tombow Adhesives for scrapbooking adhesives; 355 Satellite Blvd. Suite 300, Suwanee, GA 30024, 678-318-3344

TABLE OF CONTENTS

Page 39

Page 53

Page 66

Page 71

Page 124

Page 141

Memories

Mom and Dad-1950

"**LIFE** is not a matter of **milestones**, but of moments."

Rose Fitzgerald Kennedy

I want to introduce you to scrapbooking.

Scrapbooking, simply put, is the act of preserving memories in a creative way so that you and future generations will be able to enjoy them. Scrapbooking safely preserves personal history and allows many options for a creative hobby for people at any age.

In scrapbooks, photos are showcased with paper, card stock, embellishments, and journaling. Photos alone are just snapshots in time – we all have those photos that, when we look at them, we ask ourselves "Where was that taken?" and "Who was that?" Scrapbooking can answer the questions of who, what, why, when.

Anything that has meaning or adds interest can be added to a scrapbook page. A small piece of fabric from a child's outfit, for example, could be incorporated into a layout as a memory of an event along with a photo of the child wearing the outfit.

A scrapbook page can be as simple or complex as you want it to be. Pages can be of any size or dimension (the common ones are 8" x 8", 8-1/2" x 11", and 12" x 12"). What information you put on them is up to you. (Some of my pages, for example, have a lot of hand journaling; some have only a stenciled or rubber stamped title or a typed caption.)

The only "rule" is that you use acid- and lignin-free products. There are many products available for scrapbooking, but the vast array of products in the scrapbook or craft store can be overwhelming. This book is a guide to getting started, what basics supplies are needed, and how to use them.

My purpose for this book is to introduce anyone interested in scrapbooking to the products available; and present an array of techniques for using the products to create pages of memories. You will find 60 examples of interesting scrapbook pages to inspire you. The most widely used products and scrapbooking techniques are presented on these page examples. My hope is to inspire you and teach you so that you can enjoy the process of preserving your memories.

Rebekah Meier

TERMS

Acid-Free: Materials with a pH of 7 or greater are considered acid-free and safe for scrapbooking. Products that are labeled acid-free, including adhesives and papers, are recommended for scrapbooking since using products that are not acid-free can hasten the deterioration of photos and other paper-based memorabilia.

Archival-safe: Products labeled "archival-safe" have been tested and found to have a safe pH for use with photos. There will be no reaction with other materials.

Acrylic Craft Paints: Waterbased acrylic craft paints are available in a huge array of premixed colors in convenient plastic squeeze bottles. They are inexpensive, and a little paint goes a long way. Acrylic paint can be used to paint frames, chipboard cutouts, and brads and for stenciling and stamping.

China Marker: A wax marker that comes in many colors and can be used to write on china (hence the name). In scrapbooking, china markers are used to mark photos for cropping because the wax won't damage the photos or etch the emulsion. Find china markers at art supply stores.

Cropping: A nickname for scrapbooking. It is also the name for the process of trimming a photo to remove excess or unwanted images or make it a particular size or shape.

Embellishments: Embellishments add dimension and interest and contribute to the theme of the layout; they also may be items that are used to secure items to a page. Any acid-free embellishment can be safely used on a layout.

Embossing Powders: Embossing powders are resins that, when melted with a heat gun, create a raised surface. Commonly used with rubber stamps and watermark or clear embossing inks, they come in clear, ultra thick, and many colors.

Font: A complete set of printing type in one style, including all the letters in the alphabet (capitals and lower case), plus punctuation symbols and marks for printing in that style. Many fonts are included in computer word processing programs. Additional fonts can be purchased on the Internet.

Journaling: Writing or printing on scrapbook pages. Journaling can include a large amount of text that covers the page, a brief statement, or a single word.

Layering: Overlapping card stock, papers, and embellishments that create dimension and interest on page layouts.

Layout: A scrapbook page.

Lignin: A chemical compound found in wood-based materials such as newsprint. Materials that contain lignin will weaken and yellow with age. Lignin is non-archival. Look for products labeled "lignin-free."

Mixed Media: The combination of two or more types of materials and/or techniques within one scrapbook page or artwork.

pH Factor: The number that shows the acidity or alkalinity of a product.

Page Protector: A top- or side-loading plastic sleeve that allows finished scrapbook pages to be displayed without damage. Also called sheet protectors, the ones you use should be labeled "acid-free."

Paper Paints: Especially designed for paper, paper paints add color and dimension to scrapbook pages. They are available in different finishes (gloss, glitters, sparkles) and come in bottles with fine tips for writing. Gel paper paints can be used to tint photos.

Resist: A substance that covers or protects a surface.

Watercolor Pigments: Water soluble and sold in pots and plastic palettes, watercolors are applied with a wet brush. They are great for applying transparent washes of color and can be used for stamping.

JOURNALING

Journaling is the name given to the handwritten or computer-generated words on scrapbook pages – the thoughts and memories that describe the photo. Journaling can be as simple and brief as just names and dates or may include a relevant quote or a descriptive paragraph. To add journaling or not is a personal choice, but keep in mind that although a single picture is said to be worth a thousand words, a photo alone may not be enough to tell an entire story. A journaled scrapbook page leaves a record for generations to enjoy.

To get started, answer these questions about a photo: who? what? why? and where? Then consider adding quotes, captions, lists, notes, or children's hand prints. Journaling can be handwritten, computer-typed, or created with stickers, rub-on letters, stencils, or rubber stamps.

Remember when journaling by hand to use acid-free archival pens or markers. Archival-quality writing materials will be marked "acid-free"; check the label if you are unsure. You'll find many types of pens and markers in the scrapbook aisle.

Journaling Examples

Handwritten journaling adds a personal touch to pages.

Computer-generated journaling allows you to create a caption or block of text in a variety of fonts and type sizes.

LAYOUT BASICS

In our home decorating, we tend to embrace a particular style or styles over others. The same can be said with scrapbooking – some people, for example, like a clean and simple look, others prefer collages or an anything-goes style. As you begin creating scrapbook pages, you will develop your own style when creating a layout.

There are, however, some basic elements to consider when planning a scrapbook page. Make sure your scrapbook page consists of these elements for professional-looking results.

Page Size

Consider the size of the album and the page. Common sizes of scrapbook pages are 8" x 8", 8-1/2" x 11", and 12" x 12". Choose the size album that best suits the proportion of the photos you take or how much you want to put on a page.

Photos

The most important component on the page is usually a photo. The **photo** is the focal point of the layout. Everything else on the page is secondary and should be there only to accentuate the photo.

Background

The **background** can be a solid or decorative piece of card stock or paper that is the foundation of the scrapbook page. You can choose to have the same color throughout your album or have different colors for every page.

Mat

A **mat** frames the photo and adds texture and interest. The color you choose for your mat depends upon the background color of the page. You want the mat to contrast with the background and also complement the photo. Black is a safe bet for a mat color because it will complement most photos. If the background color of your page is black, then you need to choose a light mat color such as gray.

Title

The **title** is the statement of the theme for the page. It lets the viewer know what/who the photos are celebrating or showing. A title can be placed anywhere on the layout. Any technique, from handwriting to metal letters, can be used to create the title.

Journaling

Journaling, the writing on the page, can be simple or lengthy, typed or handwritten, or created with stencils or stickers to convey a message.

Fonts

The **font** or fonts used for the letters that create the words set the tone for the scrapbook layout. Whether in the form of stickers, chipboard cutouts, stamped metal, fabric cutouts, or any other material or written by hand, printed on a computer, or downloaded from the Internet, fonts are an important design element in scrapbooking. Combine different fonts and varieties of letters to add interest to a page.

A basic page layout (8-1/2" x 11")

Marted photo

Embellishment

Title

D a N ♥

This is one of my favorite photos of Dan. It shows that little bit of mischief he always has in his eyes. I still see it now, 15 years later, along with his dimpled smile.

Computer-generated journaling

SCRAPBOOKING PAPERS

Papers can be used as backgrounds, as mats for photos, or for layering. It can be torn, cut, printed with a computer printer, stamped, or dry embossed. Different types of paper can be used to print photos or as surfaces for journaling. Choose acid-free papers for assured longevity or spray them with an archival preservative sealer.

Here are some of the types of paper used in creating scrapbook pages:

Decorative Papers

Decorative papers are available in many designs, colors, and themes. They are found where scrapbooking supplies are sold. They are available in packs, books, or sold individually.

Card Stock

Card stock or **card paper** is heavier and thicker than decorative paper. It comes in many colors, and patterns. Card stock makes great mats for photos and as base sheets for layouts.

Transparencies

Transparencies are clear sheets of acetate commonly used with overhead projectors. Available now in the scrapbook department, they come in printed, clear, and colored designs. They can be used as overlays and backgrounds and are attached to a layout with brads or eyelets.

Decorative paper

Fabric paper

Cardstock

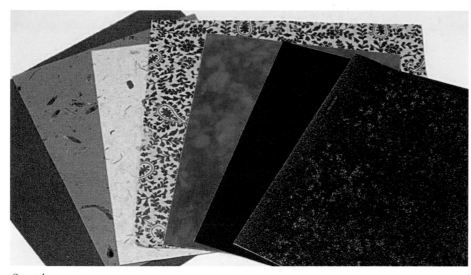

Specialty papers

Transparencies

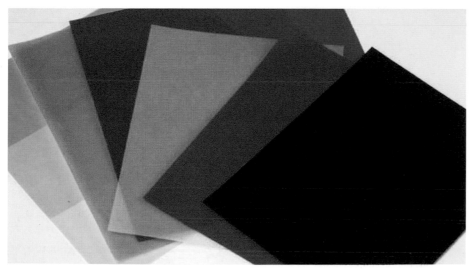

Paper vellum

Special Papers

Specialty papers offer options for creating interest, dimension, and color to layouts. Specialty papers include cork, metallic, glitter, mulberry, and handmade papers.

Fabric

Fabric papers are fabric sheets that are specially treated to have a crisp finish. Their edges won't fray, and they add texture to backgrounds, borders, and photo mats. Fabric letters, labels, tags, and pieces can be used as embellishments.

Vellum

Vellum papers are beautiful, semi-translucent, and great for layering and adding texture to pages. They are available in many colors, both plain or printed with designs or words.

Ephemera

Ephemera is the name given to all types of paper memorabilia – items like hand written correspondence, tickets, baseball cards, and print advertising.

Preservative Spray

Preservative spray is a sealer that can be used on newsprint, postcards, or memorabilia – any paper item – to neutralize the acids that makes paper deteriorate. It also protects paper from getting brittle. Follow the manufacturer's directions for use, and spray in a well-ventilated area.

ALBUMS & SCRAPBOOKS

After creating beautiful scrapbook pages, choosing the right album in which to display them is important. There are many types of albums, and they come in a variety of styles and colors. The most popular sizes are 6" square, 8" square, 12" square, and 8-1/2" x 11". I like to protect my scrapbook pages with archival sheet protectors before placing them in albums.

Post-Bound Albums

Post-bound albums are held together with screws and posts. The advantage of this type of album is that extension posts can be added when you want to add pages. Top-opening page protectors are used with this type of album.

Three-Ring Binder Albums

This is a common binder-type album — the snap-apart rings allow easy insertion and removal of pages. Three-ring albums are used with top-opening page protectors.

Photo Albums

Photo albums are a good way to organize and enjoy photos. They have slots (usually 4" x 6") for inserting photos that accommodate vertical and horizontal formats. Some photo albums have space for journaling next to the photos.

Spiral Bound or Wire-Bound Albums

Spiral albums are held together by a metal or plastic coil; wire-bound albums have a row of wire rings. This style of album is simple and inexpensive. The pages are permanently attached, however, and you can't add pages.

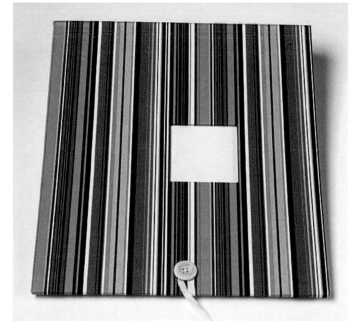

Three-Ring Binder

PAPER TRIMMERS

Paper trimmers are essential tools for the scrapbooker. You want a trimmer that is lightweight, cuts a straight line, and accommodates paper up to 12" square. Look for a trimmer with a grid system – this facilitates accurate measuring before cutting.

There are many brands and styles of trimmers available, and which one you use is a matter of personal choice. *TIP:* Ask the salesperson at the scrapbook store if they have any trimmers you can try before buying. Experiment with different varieties to see which one works best for you.
Here's some information to guide your selection:

Guillotine Trimmer

A guillotine paper trimmer has a long, sharp blade on a hinged cutting arm. Guillotine trimmers work well for cutting stacks of papers.

1

Lift cutting arm. Insert the paper flush against the top edge of the trimmer. Use the grid as a measurement guide.

2

Holding the paper with one hand, carefully pull the cutting arm downward to slice the paper.

Rotary Trimmer

Rotary paper trimmers use a wheel-type blade that slides along an arm for making straight cuts. Some rotary trimmers provide the option of inserting decorative blades to make a variety of decorative cut edges.

1

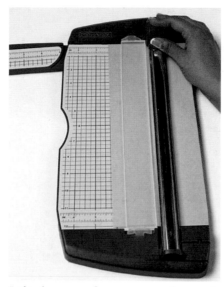

Lift the arm. Insert paper beneath the arm and flush with the top of the trimmer. Use the grid as a measurement guide.

2

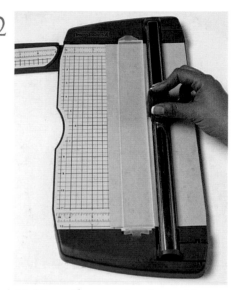

Holding the paper in place with one hand, pull the blade towards you to make the cut.

Personal Trimmer

1

Lift up the cutting arm. Make sure the blade is at the top or bottom of the trimmer.

2

Insert the paper under the arm, placing it flush with the top or bottom of the trimmer. Use the grid to ensure an accurate measurement.

3

Lower the cutting arm. Press down to move the blade downward to make the cut.

Handheld Rotary Cutter

Handheld rotary cutters are great for cutting through many layers of paper. They are also a good choice for cutting fabrics. Novelty blades are available for cutting decorative edges of papers for mats and borders.

To make straight cut, use a ruler as a guide. Always work on self-healing cutting mat to avoid damaging your work surface.

1

Place self-healing cutting mat on an even work surface.

2

Place the paper on the mat and position a ruler on the paper.

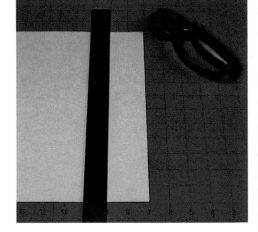

3

Run the blade of the rotary trimmer alongside the ruler, directing the trimmer away from your body.

SCISSORS

Straight Edge Scissors

There are a multitude of scissors available for cutting paper, and a good pair of scissors is a basic necessity for scrapbooking. Scissors are used for cutting papers and ribbon and for trimming stickers and embellishments.

What size scissors you use depends upon what you're cutting. Small scissors with sharp points are good for intricate cutting; scissors with long blades are good for straight cuts. Many scissors come with a comfort grip. These are a good choice when working on lengthy projects.

Scissors should be kept sharp for safety and accurate cutting. Have them professionally sharpened when they become dull. For best results, dedicate scissors to one purpose to ensure sharpness – have paper-only and fabric-only scissors.

Decorative Edge Scissors

Decorative scissors are versatile and come in many different styles. Use them for cutting photo mats or decorative elements and anywhere another design element is desired (e.g., borders, trimming around embellishments, adding detail).

You can produce different cuts from one pair of decorative scissors by flipping them over. When using decorative scissors, make small cuts and do not cut to the tip of scissors – a full cut will break the decorative pattern. Align the blades of the scissors with the previously cut section.

Decorative scissors have a limited life and will need to be replaced when the blades become dull. Occasionally cutting through wax paper or aluminum foil can help to keep them sharp.

Pictured on opposite page: This scrapbook page shows the use of two patterns of decorative scissors. The background card stock is black. A lighter color paper is layered on top of the card stock that has bottom and top edges cut with scalloped decorative edge scissors. This creates a decorative border. The title was printed on a computer and the stock was cut with decorative edge scissors. A black piece of paper was cut with the same scissors pattern to create a mat for the title. The photos were double matted with straight edges. A ribbon bow is the embellishment on the page.

True Love

1948

2001

WORKING WITH PHOTOS

Since photos preserve some of our most precious memories, it is important to learn how to store them properly and preserve them. For safekeeping, store your photos in high-quality albums or archival boxes that are acid-free and lignin-free. Using archival-quality products will ensure that your photos will be safe for many years.

Elements such as light, temperature, and humidity affect the lifespan of photos. Sunlight and fluorescent lights are the number-one enemies of photos – they cause premature fading. To prevent fading, store photos in a dark place.

The best temperature for storing a photo is 68 degrees. High temperatures can destroy the emulsion that holds the image on the photo. Places where temperatures vary from hot to cold, such as basements, attics, or garages, can cause flaking and cracking. Dampness and moist conditions can cause mold and mildew.

For safety, make copies of all your photos. Many discount stores, drug stores, and camera stores have self-service machines available for copying photos. Some machines allow to you crop the photo, make an enlargement, make the image brighter or darker, or change from color to black and white.

Photo editing software is also available for home computers. There are also on-line services that allow you to store and edit photos and order duplicate prints.

If you use a digital camera, follow the manufacturer's instructions for transferring photos from the camera to a computer. It's a good idea to always back up your camera storage media by copying the photo files to a compact disc for storage.

Photo Papers

Choose the photo paper that will give you the look (matte, gloss, or semi-gloss) you wish the photo to have. Photo papers can be found in camera departments and stores and art supply and office supply stores.

Storage & Preservation Tips

- When handling photos, hold them by their edges and keep your fingers off the image.
- Do not use anything on a photo that could scratch it, such as paper clips.
- Do not store photos in albums with adhesive pages.

Red Eye Pen

"Red eye" is caused by flash reflections in the photo subject's eyes that bounce back into the camera's lens, causing discoloration in the photo.

Use a red rye pen to remove red from eyes in photos.

Simply dab the red part of the eye in the photo with the pen – it will remove or dull the redness.

Cropping a Photo

"Cropping" is the term that refers to trimming a photo. Many times a photo contains an unwanted background or an extraneous person or visual element that distracts attention from its focal point.

When cropping, always use a copy, never the original, in case you make a mistake. Use a china marker (available in crafts and art supply stores) for marking photos, and use a paper trimmer for accurate cutting.

Supplies
- Photo
- Ruler
- Paper trimmer of your choice
- China marker

1

Determine the focal point of the photo.

2

Use a china marker and a ruler to mark the cropping lines.

3

Use paper trimmer to cut on the marked lines.

TIP: Shaped paper punches can also be used for cropping photos — large circle or square punches are great choices. For accuracy, place the punch upside down with photo inserted so you can see the image while you punch. See the section on "Paper Punches" for more information.

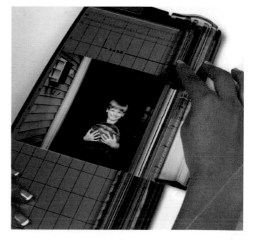

Creating a Photo Mat

Simply put, a mat is a piece of paper placed behind the photo that provides a frame. Placing a mat behind a photo gives it a finished look. Choose a mat material and color that will complement the photo. Mats can be made from card stock, vellum, handmade paper, old book pages, painted paper, or fabric. Mats can be simple or embellished with accents such as stitching (machine or hand), stickers, and metallic embellishments such as eyelets or brads. Photos can be anchored to mats with adhesives or photo corners. (Using photo corners allows you to remove the photo later, if desired.)

Supplies
- Photo
- Mat material, such as card stock
- Acid-free adhesive of choice
- Ruler
- Pencil
- Paper trimmer

Method 1

You can use this method if you are gluing the photo to the mat.

1

Determine the focal point of the photo.

2

Use a china marker and a ruler to mark the cropping lines.

3

Use paper trimmer to cut on the marked lines.

Typically, the mat is cut 1/8" or 1/4" larger on all sides than the photo. This is not a rule, however. A mat can be any size you like. In addition to photos, you can use mats to frame embellishments, titles, and journaling.

Here are two methods for making mats. **Note:** The same process can be used to create a double mat. Simply follow the steps, using an already-matted photo.

Creating a Photo Mat

Method 2

You can use this method with glue or with photo corners.

1

Measure the photo vertically and horizontally. Add 1/4" (for a 1/8" mat) or 1/2" (for a 1/4" mat) to each dimension. *Option:* Make the mat any size you want.

2

Measure and mark the dimensions on the mat material. Cut out, using a paper trimmer. Center photo on mat and adhere.

Pictured below: *The photo of Hailey is double matted. There is a thin black mat, then a wider white mat that has hand-written journaling describing Hailey. The matted photo is attached to the page with tiny metal brads in the four corners. The title on the page is done with rub-on lettering. The edge of the page around the title is antiqued by rubbing with an ink pad. Glued-on ribbons cover the seams where the various types of decorative papers join.*

Photo Tinting

Photo tinting with gel paint gives black-and-white photos an appearance reminiscent of 1950s portrait photography.

TIPS

- Less is better when applying color to photos.
- Print two copies of the photo and use one for practice.
- Use a rosy color for cheeks.
- Apply paint sparingly to start. You can always go back and add more.

Pictured on opposite page: This scrapbook page is done in a collage style with rectangles of paper used for the title, journaling and for creating decorative elements on the page. Both of the photos have been tinted. The tulip design element is done with a paper punch.

Supplies

- Photo
- Gel paint
- #0 round brush
- #0 shader brush
- Paper towels
- Scrap paper (to use as a palette)
- Water

1

Squeeze small puddles of gel paints on a scrap of paper.

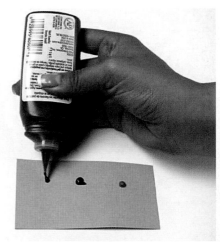

2

To apply paint, dip a brush in the puddle, gently pat the loaded brush on a paper towel, and apply color to the photo. When done, clean brushes with water.

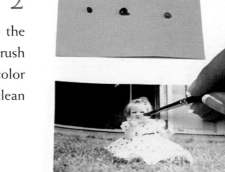

UNFORGETTABLE

Timeless

Beauty

ADHESIVES

There are many different types of adhesives for scrapbooking, including ones that set up instantly and repositionable ones that let you lift and rearrange page elements. The adhesive you choose depends upon what you're gluing. For example, if you are matting a photo, you might use a dispenser, double-stick tape, photo sticker squares, or a glue stick – all would be appropriate choices. Some embellishments require a more durable bond. Adhesive dots, liquid paper glue, and foam mounting tape are good choices for added strength. Specialty papers such as vellum require special adhesives.

Look for adhesives that say they are **archival-safe** meaning there is no reaction between them and the other materials such as paper or photos; **acid-free** because these types of adhesives won't weaken the paper or the photos; **acrylic-based** because they won't bleed through the paper; and **lignin-free** and won't yellow when bonded.

> **TIP**
> When cutting adhesive-backed products, use scissors with a non-stick finish.

Liquid Paper Glue

Liquid paper glue comes in a bottle, stick, or pen applicator. It's fast-drying and great for adhering embellishments and trims such as ribbon to pages.

> **TIP**
> Set-up time on this type of adhesive allows a short time for repositioning, if needed. It's a good idea to determine the placement and mark the spot with a pencil before gluing.

1

Apply a dab of glue to the back of the element.

2

Position the element on the paper or page. Press in place.

Adhesive Dots

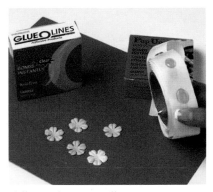

Adhesive dots on a roll.

Adhesive dots are instant-bonding, double-sided adhesive dots made of glue. They come in many sizes and thicknesses on sheets and rolled strips. Adhesive dots provide a permanent, strong hold for photographs, card stock, and lightweight embellishments. You can also use them to adhere glitter.

1

Press item you want to adhere on an adhesive dot.

2

Gently pull the item to lift it and the adhesive dot. Press the item in place.

Glue Stick

A glue stick is a convenient, retractable paste adhesive in a tube. It can be used to affix photos and paper.

1

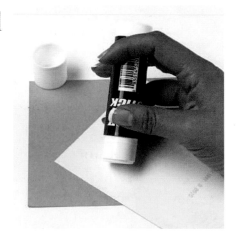

Turn over element. Apply glue to all edges.

2

Turn over and press on mat or background.

Spray Adhesive

Spray adhesive is a quick option when you require flexibility and a non-wrinkling bond. It is great for bonding sheer or transparent materials like vellum or substances such as glitter to a layout.

CAUTION: Always follow the manufacturer's instructions. Avoid inhaling the fumes. Work in a well-ventilated area.

1

Completely cover the back of vellum with adhesive spray.

2

Position vellum, adhesive side down. Press in place with your fingers.

Vellum Tape

Vellum tape is specially formulated to "disappear" on most vellum papers. Vellum tape comes on a roll with a backing carrier strip.

1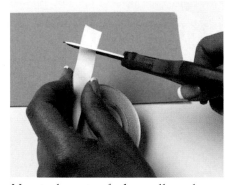

Unwind part of the roll and cut small squares of tape with scissors.

2

Apply tape pieces, with carrier pieces attached, to the back of the vellum.

Pictured on opposite page: There are two vellum panels that have been taped down with vellum tape. Stickers were used for the lettering on vellum. A photo turn adds a decorative element by holding down one corner of the vellum panel. A metal clip is used for decoration on the bottom vellum panel.

3

Remove the carrier pieces from the backs of the tape pieces..

4

Position taped vellum on paper and press to adhere.

Tape Applicator

A tape applicator applies a thin, even film of sticky tape that creates an instant bond. There are two types: permanent and repositionable. Choose the best one for your task.

1

Apply tape to the back of the element by pulling the tape applicator across it.

2

Turn over, position, and press to adhere.

Double-Sided Tape

Double-sided (or double-stick) tape is sticky on both sides; one side is covered with a protective film to prevent it from sticking to itself. It's great for adhering photos, borders, and lightweight embellishments.

1

Pull the desired amount of tape from the dispenser. Place the sticky side of the tape on the surface.

2

Peel away the protective film from the tape.

3

Position and press to adhere.

TIP
Use double-sided tape to apply small beads or glitter to scrapbook pages.

Adhesive Foam Dots

Self-adhesive, double-sided foam dots are perfect for adding dimension to a layout. They come on sheets and have a protective film on each side.

2

Apply foam dots, sticky side down, to the back of the element.

1

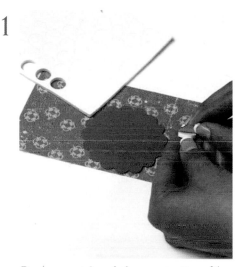

Peel one side of the protective film from foam dots.

3

Pull off the remaining protective film from the dots.

TIP
Foam dots come in a variety of sizes. Choose a size that corresponds to the size of the element, e.g., for tiny dimensional elements, use small dots. On larger elements, use more than one dot.

4

Turn over, position, and press element on paper.

Foam Mounting Tape

Foam mounting tape provides dimension for photos or accents. Available in rolls or shapes, it is double-sided and strong for a permanent mount.

1

Cut tape into pieces as needed. Turn the element you want to tape to the backside. Peel film from one side of mounting tape pieces and apply to element.

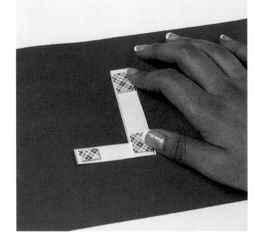

2

Remove remaining film from tape.

3

Position element and press into place.

Photo Corners

Photo corners are small triangular tabs that are used as anchors to attach photos or paper pieces to layouts. Some photo corners have adhesive backing; others require moisture for adhesion or the application of an adhesive. Available in a variety of colors, photo corners can be permanently attached as a decorative element or they can be attached to the mat or the page, allowing easy removal of the photo or other memorabilia.

Supplies
- Photo corners
- Photo mat (if desired)
- Photo
- Adhesive (if attaching corners to photo)

1

To attach a photo corner permanently to a photo, apply adhesive to corners of photo.

2

Apply photo corners to the photo over the adhesive.

3

Most photo corners have glue on the back – simply moisten the glue with water and mount. For added security you can place a small amount of glue on the back instead.

PAPER PUNCHES

Punched shapes provide great accents for pages, and punches can be used to crop photos. Paper punches create both a positive image (the cutout piece) and a negative image (the silhouette of the cutout). Both can be used for borders and embellishments – simply attach with an adhesive or with fasteners such as brads or eyelets.

Handheld hole punches look like pliers. They can be used to punch designs or decorative accents or to make starter holes for brads or embellishments. In addition to the familiar geometric shapes like circles, squares, and triangles, hand-held punches are available with designs such as stars, hearts, and flowers.

Decorative punches are made from plastic and metal and come in many styles and sizes. Decorative punches have very sharp, moveable blades inside a cylinder. You press on the punch to create the design.

TIP: Sharpen a dull punch by punching aluminum foil or wax paper.

Pictured opposite page: On this scrapbook page, the flowers have been created with two paper punches – a flower shape and a circle. The pieces are layered and attached to the page with a metal brad as the center. A hand-held punch was used to punch the small circles in the two bottom corners of the page. Other elements on the page include chipboard letters spelling "Love;" rub-on letters were used for "your smile;" photo corners as decorative elements on the photo; decorative stamps on the title section of the page.

Handheld Punches

Supplies
- Punch
- Paper

Insert the paper on the punch, positioning as desired. Press the handles to punch the design.

Decorative Punches

Place the punch on a stable work surface. Slide paper in the slit of the punch and position as desired. Press down on the top of the punch to cut the paper and make the design.

There is a wide variety of designs available.

cindy and katrina

LOVE YOUR Smile

Corner Punches

As their name implies, corner punches are specially designed for punching corners. They also can be used to make cuts in mats to hold photos in place without an adhesive (like photo corners do) and to add decorative detail to a layout.

1

Place the punch on a stable work surface. Align the photo (or paper) with the marks on the punch.

2

Press the punch to cut off the corner and create the shape.

Supplies
- Corner punch
- Photo

TIP

Turning over the punch to check the placement ensures accuracy when punching corners.

Using a Punch to Crop a Photo

A large-shape punch such as a circle or square makes cropping photos quick and easy. If you work with the punch upside down you'll be able to see the placement of the punched shape on the photo.

1

Turn punch upside down on a stable work surface. Slide the photo into the slit of the punch with the image side facing you.

2

Press down on the punch to make the cut.

3

Remove the photo to reveal the punched shape.

TEMPLATES

Templates are sheets of brass, chipboard, or plastic with cutout shapes or letters. The shapes can be traced and cut with scissors or a craft knife to create elements for a layout, including items such as tags and envelopes.

With an embossing stylus, templates can be used for dry embossing.

TIP
Change blades on your craft knife often to ensure accurate cuts.

Pictured on opposite page: The letters were made with templates. The journaling was done on a computer. Ribbon forms a decorative border at the bottom of the page under the title.

Letter Templates

Supplies
- Template • Paper
- Pencil • Craft knife
- Self-healing cutting mat

1 Position template on paper. (When cutting out letters, heavier paper or card stock is easier to work with.) Use a pencil to trace the letter shapes.

2 Cut out the letter shapes along the traced lines, using a craft knife.

3 Arrange the letters to make words or titles.

Kauffman Family

It is not very often that we all get together. I like this photo because looking back so much has changed. Thankfully we are all still here. It makes me laugh at how our hair looks, but wish I were still that thin! This photo was taken at mom and dad's house in 1993 when my sister Cindy came for a visit.

FAMILY

Shape Templates

You can use shape templates to cut mats for photos, paper shapes for layering, or frames for journaling. Simple shapes can be cut out with scissors. More complex shapes may require a craft knife.

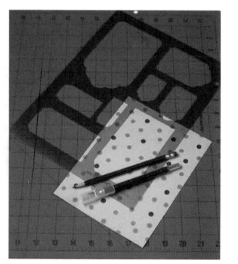

Supplies
- Template
- Scissors or craft knife
- Self-healing cutting mat
- Pencil
- Paper or card stock

1

Position the template on the paper. Use a pencil to trace around the shape.

2

Cut along the traced lines with scissors.

3

The cutout shape, ready for your layout.

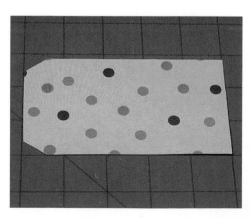

Cropping a Photo with a Template

Shape templates such as ovals, circles, or squares can be used to crop photos.

Supplies
- Template
- Photo
- Scissors
- China marker
- Tissue

1

Place the template on the photo over the area to be cropped. Trace around the shape with a china marker.

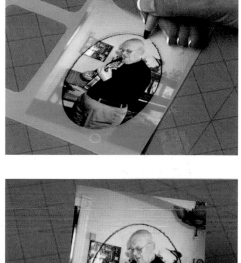

2

Cut along the traced line with scissors.

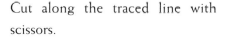

3

Use a tissue to rub away any remaining traces of the china marker. Mount photo on scrapbook page.

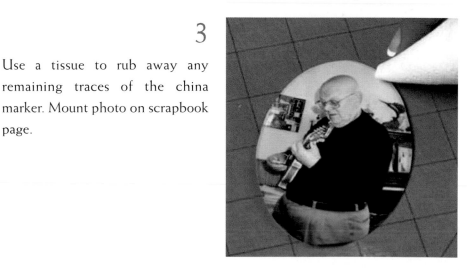

STAMPS & INKS

Stamps are versatile tools that can be used to add color, texture, motifs, or letters to scrapbook pages. It is easy to create custom papers by stamping plain card stock or paper. When stamping, you can coordinate ink or paint colors with photos and decorative papers.

Stamps can be made of rubber or foam. Rubber stamps are available mounted or unmounted. Generally, mounted stamps are easier for beginners to use. Foam stamps, which are made completely of foam, are flexible and work better than rubber stamps on uneven or curved surfaces.

The type of ink you use depends on the surface and the effect you want. **Pigment inks** are thick and opaque. Because they are slow drying, they are a good choice for heat embossing. Pigment inks are not recommended for glossy or coated papers.

Dye inks are fast drying on all types of papers and create a crisp image. Dye inks are a good choice for glossy and coated papers. They can be used for embossing as long as the ink is wet enough to accept embossing powders. Dye inks are also used for distressing or aging papers and photos.

Solvent inks are archival and fast drying. They can be used on all surfaces, including non-porous surfaces such as metal, plastic, glass, and transparencies. Solvent inks will not smear when used with watercolors and watercolor markers.

Watermark inks are used for embossing and as resists for chalk and pigment powders. When rubber stamping, watermark inks leave a clear mark over which embossing powders or chalks can be applied. Embossing powders should be heat set; chalks should be sprayed with a fixative to set the color. Similar to watermark ink, **embossing ink** is thick, slow drying and used for heat embossing. It may be clear or have a slight pink tint.

When buying ink pads, it's a good idea to purchase a re-inker bottle. You can use re-inker to refresh the ink pad or to add aging or color to paper.

Basic Stamping with Ink

1

Lay the stamp on a flat surface with the right side of the stamp facing upward. Load the stamp by dabbing or patting the ink pad on the stamp.

2

With the inked image facing downward, place the stamp firmly on the paper and press. Do not rock stamp. Lift the stamp to reveal the image.

Pictured on opposite page: A stamp was used to create a decorative design on pink paper. The square stamped design was cut out. An "S" letter sticker was applied to this square; then the square was mounted to the page. Pieces of striped and flowered decorative paper were attached to scrapbook page to create decorative elements. Hand journaling was done below the photo to record the date of photo. The title "Cherish the moment" is rub-on lettering directly on the background paper.

Sarah 1997

S

Cherish
THE MOMENT

Watercolor Stamping

You can use watercolor paints – either watercolor pigment pots or palette (pan) paints – for stamping, instead of ink. Two or three colors may be applied to a stamp to achieve a variegated image.

Using two or more stamps with similar images, you can create interesting backgrounds, borders, or decorations.

Supplies
- 2 rubber stamps
- Paint brush
- Watercolor paints
- Water
- Paper or card stock
- Paper towels
- Wet wipes

1

Wet brush with water. (Using less water makes for a clearer image.) Dip brush into watercolor pigment.

2

Use the brush to load watercolors on the rubber stamps. You can paint various colors on the stamp to create a variegated image. Clean the brush with water between color changes to avoid a muddy look.

3

Randomly stamp images on paper. Several images can be stamped from one application of color. Clean brush with water. Clean stamp with a wet wipe.

Pictured opposite page: *The flowered strip of paper on the right side of the page was created by stamping the image with watercolors. The images were stamped randomly on a piece of white card stock then cut into rectangle and mounted to page.*

49

Heat Embossing

Heat embossing creates a raised image of the stamp on paper. An image is stamped, then sprinkled with embossing powder, and heated with a heat embossing gun, which melts the powder. A heat embossing gun is a hand-held tool that looks like a hair dryer. But don't let the resemblance fool you – they're not the same. **Never** try to use a hair dryer for heat embossing.

Watermark, pigment, or embossing ink can be used to stamp images for heat embossing. Embossing powder is available in clear or colors. You can use a tinted inkpad for most colors of embossing powder, causing very little visual difference in the color of the embossing powder. You can use a tinted inkpad with clear embossing powder to achieve a color also. If you want a solid, intense color result, such as solid black, it is better to use a colored powder to get the color intensity.

Pictured on opposite page: embossing has been used to create the flower at top right of page and for the title "MEL." A flower stamp was used with clear embossing ink and stamped onto white paper. Pink embossing powder was used. The flower design was then cut out and attached to page. A button and ribbon were used to embellish the flower. For the letters, letter stamps were used with clear embossing ink and stamped onto colored decorative paper. Clear embossing powder was used. The letters were cut out and attached to page. A strip of decorative paper, rickrack, and a "100% girl" sticker are embellishments to the page.

Supplies
- Ink pad • Paper or card stock
- Stamp of your choice
- Embossing heat gun
- Embossing powder

1

Load the stamp with ink and stamp image on paper.

2

Pour a generous amount of embossing powder over the stamped image. Embossing powder tends to stick to places you have touched so be careful, or rub the paper with an anti-static cloth before pouring on the powder.

3

Shake off the excess embossing powder onto a sheet of paper. Use the paper to pour the excess embossing powder back into the jar.

4

Use the heat gun to set the embossing powder. Hold the heat gun several inches from the image. Keep the gun moving with circular motions so you do not overheat one spot. Almost immediately, you will see the embossing powder melt to form the shiny image. This should take about 30 seconds. Let cool before handling.

Shadow Stamping

Shadow stamping is the technique of layering one stamped image with two or more designs. A solid shape such as a square or circle is stamped to create a background for an image stamp. The ink used for the solid shape should be a lighter color than the ink used for the image.

Supplies
- 2 stamps – 1 solid shape, 1 image
- 2 pigment ink pads in contrasting colors
- Paper or card stock

1

Load the solid stamp with the lighter color pigment ink.

2

Press the stamp on the paper or card stock.

3

Load the image stamp with the other (darker) color ink.

4

Press the image stamp on the solid stamped image. This can be done while the ink from the first stamping is still wet or you can allow the first ink to dry.

Pictured on opposite page: *Shadow stamping was done for the number "1" on the bottom of page. The images were stamped on a piece of yellow paper, then cut out and mounted to page. The letter "M" was done with the heat embossing technique. The edge of the yellow paper on which the photo is mounted has been antiqued with ink. A piece of ribbon holds tiny safety pins to which tags have been attached for journaling. The tag was cut with a punch.*

Kissing Stamps Technique

The kissing stamps technique uses two stamps to create a design that is an image within a shape. The image stamp is used to remove the ink from the loaded solid stamp before stamping on paper.

Supplies
- Ink pad with pigment or dye ink
- Paper or card stock
- Solid geometric shape stamp
- Small image stamp

1

Load the solid stamp with ink.

2

Press the image stamp on the inked solid stamp. (This removes ink from the solid stamp, creating a negative image.) Set aside the image stamp.

3

Press the solid stamp on the paper or card stock. Lift to reveal the image.

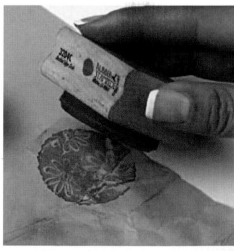

Pictured opposite page: The kissing technique was used for the dots under the title word "oh." For an extra distressed effect, the piece of paper was crumbled then ironed flat before stamping on it. After stamping, the paper was cut into a rectangle and glued to page. The title "oh" are 4" chipboard letters that have been rubbed with several colors of ink from an inkpad. Under the title is a pocket that contains hidden journaling. The flowers on the top right are die cuts.

Stamping with Paint

Opaque paper paint and acrylic craft paint can be used for stamping instead of ink. Paint works especially well with rubber stamps that have bold, heavy design lines. You can stamp on any kind of paper (plain or decorative) or on card stock. Use a paint brush to load the stamp with paint. Wash the stamp immediately after use with warm water.

Supplies
- Opaque paper paint
- Paper
- Stamp
- Paint brush
- Palette or scrap of card stock (to use as a palette)

1

Squeeze a small puddle of paint on a scrap of card stock or a palette.

2

Using a paint brush, load the stamp with paint.

3

Stamp the image on paper.

Pictured opposite page: The title "MATT" was stamped with purple paper paint. The letters were stamped onto printed decorative paper. The piece was cut out and mounted to a piece of lavender paper that was cut with decorative edge scissors. Brads hold this piece in place on the page. The journaling tags on the right were cut out with a punch.

Masking with Tape

Masking with tape, when paired with random stamping, creates a patterned paper with a defined border. Use this technique to create mats or frames for photos or journaling. It's also nice for backgrounds.

The same technique can be used to mask out any area where you don't want the random stamped design. Before stamping, you can place masking tape over any areas where you want to remain the paper color.

Be sure to use a low tack ("safe release") masking tape and to remove it promptly.

Supplies
- Paint *or* ink • Stamp
- Paper
- Paint brush (if using paint)
- Low tack masking tape
- Ruler • Pencil
- Decorative scissors

1

Determine the size of the stamped area you want to create. Measure and mark with a pencil and ruler.

2

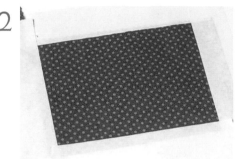

Apply low tack masking tape along the marked lines.

3

Load a stamp and randomly press the stamp over the masked-off area. Stamp some of the images so that part of the image is on the masking tape, resulting in a partial image on the paper. Blot any excess paint with a paper towel. Let dry completely. *Note: Here the paper was first painted with a gel paint and allowed to dry before stamping. This changes the color of the paper and adds a layer of dimension and transparency to the design.*

4

Remove the tape. The painted and stamped area can be cut out and mounted to page. You can create a double mat effect by trimming the masked-off area with decorative scissors, trimming outside the stamped area to pick up some of the solid color.

Pictured opposite page: The masking technique was used to create the mat behind the photo. The striped yellow decorative paper was painted with green gel paint, then masked off and randomly stamped with blue paint. After tape was removed, decorative edged scissors in a scalloped design cut just outside the masked off area to pick up some of the yellow paper.

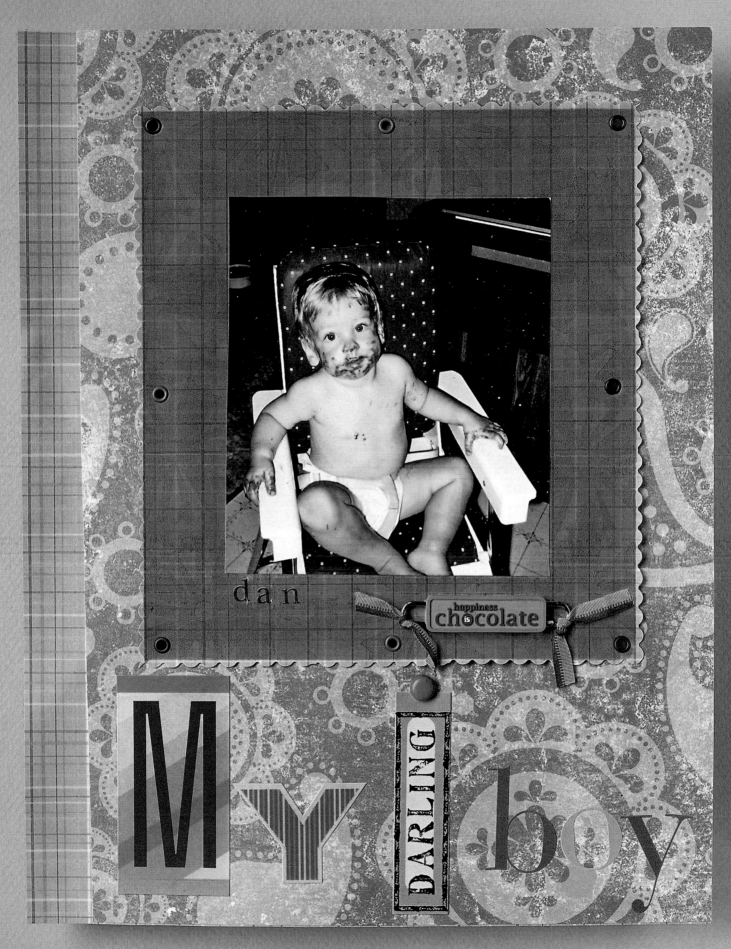

dan

happiness is chocolate

MY DARLING boy

Resist Embossed Stamping

Stamping, embossing, and sponging are combined in this technique. A stamped image is embossed with clear powder, then the paper is sponged with pigment ink. The embossed stamped image resists the ink, but the paper around it takes on the ink color. If you use printed decorative paper, you'll see the paper design through the embossed image and sponged ink.

Supplies
- Ink pad with watermark or embossing ink
- Pigment ink
- Clear embossing powder
- Embossing heat gun
- Rubber stamp
- Paper (In the photo and scrapbook page example, decorative paper with printed writing is used.)
- Cosmetic sponge

1

Load rubber stamp with watermark ink or embossing ink.

3

Pour clear embossing powder on the stamped image. Pour excess powder back into the jar.

5

Sponge pigment ink across embossed image and onto the paper. The embossed image will resist the ink, creating a watermark effect. The entire piece of paper can be inked or you can ink just the area around the stamped image.

2

Stamp the image on paper.

4

Use the heat gun to set the embossing powder, holding the heat gun several inches from the image and moving the heat gun back and forth. You will see the powder melt and become a clear, shiny image. You will be able to see the paper through the stamped image.

Pictured opposite page: The resist technique was done for the panel on right. The left edge of the paper was hand torn. The journaling was done on vellum and attached to panel with vellum tape. Machine stitching was done around the photo.

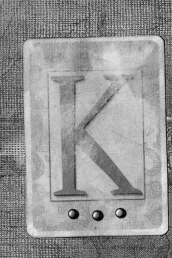

KATE

Friends like Flowers
give pleasure
just by being.

PAINTS & OTHER COLORANTS

Acrylic Paint Backgrounds

You can use acrylic craft paints to create customized painted paper for backgrounds. The paints can be used straight from the bottle or thinned for a watercolor effect, and very little paint is needed. Simply apply the paint with a brush or use household items such as a crumpled piece of plastic wrap or a sea sponge to pounce the paint on paper for a fun effect.

Supplies
- Acrylic craft paint
- Paper
- Stiff-bristle paint brush
- Scrap of paper, palette, or disposable plate
- Paper towels

1

Squeeze a small puddle of paint on a disposable plate, paper scrap, or palette.

2

Dip the tips of the brush bristles in the paint and pounce the loaded brush on a paper towel to remove almost all of the paint.

3

Randomly brush paint on the paper, allowing some of the paper to show through. Reload brush if more coverage is desired.

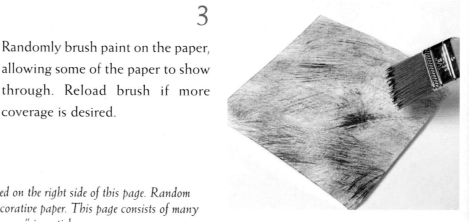

Pictured on opposite page: Acrylic paint has been used on the right side of this page. Random dabs of light-colored paint were used to accent the decorative paper. This page consists of many layered strips of decorative paper. The title "Sweet Success" is a sticker.

vicky

Sweet Success

Stenciling with Paint

Stencils are a great way to add lettering for titles or repeating motifs for backgrounds to pages. Made of brass, chipboard, or plastic with cutout designs, stencils are reusable and inexpensive.

You can use acrylic paint, stencil paints or gels, or ink for stenciling. The size of the stencil brush used depends on the size of the stencil openings. It's best to use a small stencil brush on stencils with small openings; larger brushes can be used on stencils with larger openings.

Supplies
- Acrylic craft paint
- Stencil
- Paper
- Stencil brush
- Paper towels
- Paper plate, palette, or scrap paper
- Low-tack masking tape

1

Squeeze a small puddle of paint on a paper plate, palette, or scrap of paper. Position stencil on paper. Tape in place with low-tack tape.

2

Dip the tips of the stencil brush in the paint. Pounce the loaded brush on a paper towel to remove most of the paint.

3

Gently tap the paint through the openings of the stencil. Carefully lift the stencil to reveal the design.

Pictured on opposite page: *Paint was used in two places on this page. The printed background paper was stenciled with magenta flowers. The mat under photo and the rectangle of paper under the journaling has edges that have been accented with acrylic paint applied randomly with a brush.*

FIRST
Day of
school

Mattie
KindeRgarteN
1994

Pigment Powders

Pigment powders are finely ground, highly concentrated colors. They can be brushed on designs that have been stamped with watermark ink. They can also be combined with paint, ink, or other colorants to create shimmering effects. Use this technique to create borders, titles, and accents.

Supplies
- Pigment powder
- Ink pad with watermark ink
- Paper
- Stamp
- Small soft brush
- Spray sealer
- *Optional:* Tissue

1

Load stamp with watermark ink.

2

Stamp image on paper.

3

While the ink is wet, use a small brush to apply pigment powder to the stamped image by lightly brushing over image. Shake off excess powder and put back in the jar. Allow to dry. Remove any stray bits of powder from the paper with the brush or a tissue. Spray lightly with sealer.

Pictured opposite: The letter "H" has been treated with pigment powders. Watermark ink was applied to the large chipboard letter and pigment powder was brushed over the letter. The flower on the left is a silk flower with a bottle cap center. An initial sticker is placed in the middle of the bottle cap.

Pens & Markers

Leafing Pens are metallic ink in an easy-to-use form. They come in silver, gold, bronze, and copper. Use them to highlight the edges of paper cutouts or to print titles, to color metal accents, or to create freestyle stripes.

Markers are great for journaling, adding color to rubber stamped images, and anywhere where extra color is needed. Look for waterbased markers that can be blended with a special blender marker especially designed for that purpose.

Gel Pens are great for journaling. They are available in numerous colors and point sizes and are fast drying. They are available in metallic, opaque, and fluorescent colors and work well on vellum.

Adding a Metallic Edge

Supplies
- Leafing pen
- Paper cutout

Prepare the pen for use according to the package instructions. Drag the tip of the pen along the edge of the paper to make a border of metallic color. Allow to dry.

Pictured opposite: Leaf pens have been used to enhance the metal letters, "and" and to color the plastic hinge and square embellishments on the title "artful." A colored marker was used to add a magenta border around the bottom layer piece of the tag made for the "artful" title as well as the strip of paper under the "enduring" journaling. The papers used for the "artful" title and mat were torn by hand. A piece of brown kraft paper was crumpled then smoothed before stamping the title "artful."

ENDURING (en-door´ing) 1. lasting; permanent 2. continuing on until the end

ARTFUL

SCALE OF STATUTE MILES

160

240

60

80

0

ARCTIC REGIONS

Dimensional Paper Paints

Especially designed for use with paper, paper paints add color and dimension to scrapbook pages. They come in bottles with fine applicator tips so they can be applied directly from the bottle. You can also use the tips to create raised letters, to make dots of color for borders, or to highlight stickers.

Paper paint can also be squeezed on a plate or palette and applied to paper with a brush, sea sponge, or piece of crumpled plastic wrap to create custom effects.

Supplies
- Paper paint, choice of colors
- Paper

Use the tips of the paint bottles to write or doodle designs directly on paper. Allow paint to dry completely.

Pictured: Paper paint was used to make the large random doodle on the background paper. The edge of the square of paper that has the journaling has been accented with acrylic paint dabbed on with a stencil brush. The "F" is chipboard that has been stamped with a random design.

Spray Paints

Aerosol spray paints, available in many colors and finishes such as metallic, translucent, glitter, or antiquing, are a quick way to add color and texture to embellishments or papers for backgrounds and borders. Spray paints labeled "paper finishes" are acid-free and safe for photos.

CAUTION: When working with aerosol products, wear a mask that covers your nose and mouth and spray in a well-ventilated area. Protect adjacent areas from overspray.

Supplies
- Spray paint
- Paper

Spray paint on paper lightly or heavily, for desired effect. TIP: Test your technique on a scrap piece of paper before spraying your project.

Pictured: *The letters in the title "Life" have been spray painted with a transparent "stained glass" type of spray paint. The photo turn has also been spray painted. The other lettering on the page is stickers. Cork paper is the mat under the photo. Eyelets, a metal clip, and photo corners are the other embellishments to the page.*

Chalks

Decorative chalks add dimensional color to images when you use them for shading and highlighting. With a small amount of chalk, you can add subtle accents to paper, paper elements, die cuts, or embossed accents.

Available in cake form, chalks can be applied with a sponge applicator or a fingertip. Use a chalk eraser to remove unwanted chalk marks.

Set chalk and prevent it from transferring to other areas by applying a spray fixative. Follow the manufacturer's instructions and work in a well-ventilated area.

Supplies
- Chalk
- Paper
- Applicator
- *Optional:* Spray fixative

1

Load applicator with chalk by rubbing the applicator over the surface.

2

Add color to an area by applying chalk with a swirling motion.

3

Or add highlights to paper edges by pulling the applicator along the edges of the paper. Chalk looks especially nice on torn paper edges.

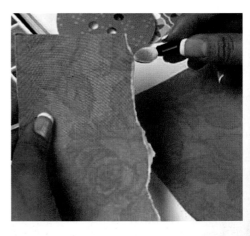

Pictured opposite: *Chalk has been used to color the chipboard star as well as enhance the edges of the background paper and the mats under the two photos. The photo at bottom left is covered with a piece of vellum with printed handwriting on it. The vellum covered photo and mat are attached to page with eyelets at corners. The title "Washington" and the journaling are stickers.*

WASHINGTON

Jefferson Memorial, 2005.

"Who travels 4 love finds a thousand miles not longer than one."
Japanese Proverb

Do not go where the path may lead, go instead where there is no path, and leave a trail.

Metallic Rub-On Waxes

Metallic rub-on waxes add shimmering color and dramatic highlights to papers (they look great on crumpled paper) and fabric and to embellishments like brads, chipboard cutouts, or clay pieces.

Apply rub-on waxes with a sponge-tip applicator or your finger, working in circular motion or in short strokes. Spray with a matte preservative to seal and to assure acid-free preservation. Non-porous surfaces should be sprayed with sealer to set the color and prevent smearing.

Supplies
- Metallic rub-on waxes
- Plastic or metallic embellishments
- Paper
- Sponge tip applicator

1

Load the applicator by rubbing it across the surface of the metallic wax.

2

Apply color to paper with a swirling motion.

3

Or rub across the surface of the embellishment. Your finger can also be used to apply the wax.

Pictured opposite page: Metallic rub-on waxes have been applied to the edges of the photo mats and the piece of paper with the computer lettering "reminisce." Metallic rub-on wax also was applied to the plastic letters "the" at top of page. Machine stitching is used as a border around the red paper rectangle under the matted photos. A gel pen was used to do the hand journaling on the strip of green paper.

THE HOUSE

rem·in·isce
to think about, usually with fondness

RIBBONS, LACE & FIBER TRIMS

Attaching Ribbon with Staples

Ribbons and fibers are a great way to add color, pattern, and dimension to a layout. They can be tied in bows, wrapped around accents, or used as borders, to create flowers, or to attach small trinkets. Find them in crafts, fabric, needlework, and scrapbook stores.

Printed or plain, ribbons come in a vast array of colors, widths, and textures. Some popular choices are satin, grosgrain, and organza. Lace and other flat trims like twill tape can be used in the same ways as ribbons. Simply glue, clip, staple, tape, or attach with brads to the scrapbook page.

Fibers such as jute, yarn, and raffia can be tied or adhered with glue.

Supplies
- Stapler
- Ribbon
- Card stock
- Scissors

1

Cut ribbon to desired length with scissors.

2

Fold ribbon position on card stock. Staple through both layers of ribbon and the card stock to hold in place.

3

The staple adds a metallic accent.

Pictured opposite: *A piece of folded 1/4" ribbon has been used to accent the triple-matted photo. The strip of decorative paper on the left that runs under the photos has been attached to the background paper with machine stitching.*

to much fun!

Danny
Summer 1987

Glued Ribbons with Ends Showing

One way to glue ribbon to paper accents is to allow the ends to extend past the edges of the paper.

1

Position the ribbon with the cut end extending over the edge of the paper. Mark the position of the ribbon with a light pencil mark.

2

Apply glue to the paper and press the ribbon in place over the glue.

Attaching Ribbon with Brads

When you use brads to attach ribbon to a layout, the brads hold the ribbon in place and add color and dimension. A small hole punch is used to make holes for the brads.

1

Position the ribbon on a piece of card stock. Use a hole punch to punch a hole through the card stock and the ribbon.

2

Insert the brad through the hole, spread the prong, and flatten them against the back of the paper.

Glued Ribbons with Hidden Ends

Hiding the cut ends of ribbon trims gives paper pieces a tailored, finished look. You'll need a piece of ribbon that's about an inch longer than the paper piece you're wrapping the ribbon around. A drop of glue ensures the ribbon will stay in place on the front side.

1

Cut ribbon to size with scissors and determine how it will be positioned on the card stock. Place a small line of glue where ribbon will be placed.

2

Place the ribbon on the card stock over the glue.

Supplies
- Ribbon
- Liquid adhesive
- Clear tape
- Card stock
- Scissors

3

Turn over the card stock. Fold over one end of the ribbon and secure the end with tape. Fold over the other end of the ribbon and secure with tape.

Fibers

Fibers such as yarn or string are colorful, dimensional additions to scrapbook pages. Thread them through holes or eyelets or wrap them around card stock pieces, cutout embellishments, or paper tags for instant texture. Fibers can be tied, braided, knotted, or looped.

Supplies
- Fibers
- Tag
- Scissors

1

Cut desired amounts of fibers.

2

Fold fibers in half lengthwise. Slip the folded end through the hole in the tag.

3

Place the ends of the fibers through the loop formed by the folded end. Pull to secure. Trim ends of fibers with scissors to desired length.

Pictured opposite: At the bottom of this page, a large eyelet creates a hole through which narrow metallic fiber has been threaded. The fiber wraps around the edge of paper, through hole, and is tied at front. The piece of paper with the sticker letters "attitude" has been hand torn and the edges have been antiqued with ink. Snaps attach the matted photo. A small length of metallic fiber is wrapped around one of the snaps for decoration.

BIG

aTTiTuDe

Sarah + Katie, 1986

HARDWARE

Brads, buttons, eyelets, photo turns, zippers, buckles, charms, bottle caps, and clips are just some of the hardware embellishments that can be used to accent and add interest to any scrapbook layout. Hardware embellishments can also attach paper and other elements to a page.

Brads

Using a Hole Punch with Brads

Brads come in many sizes, shapes, and colors; some have letters or flowers on them. Brads can be used by themselves as decorative elements and are a great way to attach page elements such as frames, vellum, titles, journaling, and cutouts or items such as hinges or photo turns.

After making a small hole, the prongs of the brad are inserted through the hole, opened, and flattened against the back of the paper to secure. For accuracy, mark the placement of the hole with a faint pencil mark.

1

Use a small-hole paper punch to make a hole through all the layers of paper that is large enough for the prongs of the brad to go through.

2

Insert the brad through the hole.

3

Turn over the paper. Open and flatten ("butterfly") the brad's prongs.

Using a Pushpin with Brads

This brad technique can be used to attach any kind of embellishment (frames, tags, etc.) to a layout.

Supplies
- Brads
- Pushpin
- Paper
- Embellishment

1

Use a pushpin to poke a hole into the paper (or other material) where the brad is to be inserted.

2

Insert the brad through the hole in the tag.

3

Turn over the paper. Open and flatten ("butterfly") the brad's prongs.

Attaching Label Holders with Brads

Label holders provide a place to slip a title or caption to label a page. The ones originally designed for mounting on wood have holes for attaching them with screws. Brads are an ideal way to attach label holders: simply use the holes intended for the screws.

1

Position the label holder on the card stock. Use a pushpin to make a hole through the screw hole of the label holder.

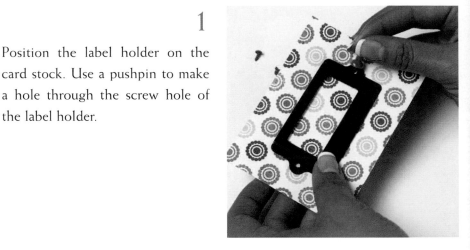

2

Slip the prongs of the brad through the hole, attaching the label holder. Turn over the card stock and spread and flatten the prongs of the brad.

Supplies
- Card stock
- Label holder
- Pushpin
- Brads (one for each hole in the label holder)

3

Repeat the process to insert a brad on the other side of the label holder.

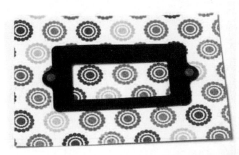

Pictured on opposite page: *Below photo a loopy brad has been attached to the page. A ribbon is looped through the brad and the ends glued to the back of the page. Three brads on each side of the double-matted photo call attention to the photo. The chipboard letter "K" has been painted with acrylic paint. The title "Cherish" was done with rub-on lettering. The lettering at the bottom is a sticker.*

August & Elsie 1950

TOGETHERNESS (to-geth'-ur-nes) 1. the spending of much time together, resulting in a more unified bond

Eyelets

Eyelets are metal rings that reinforce holes in paper or fabric. They come in many shapes, colors, and sizes. Use eyelets on scrapbook pages to join elements together, to make decorative holes on the page, and to attach ribbons and fibers.

Eyelets must be set (attached) with an eyelet setter that flattens the back and secures them in place.

Supplies
• Setting tool set *or* handheld all-in-one punch
• Self-healing cutting mat
• Eyelets   • Paper

Pictured on opposite page: *Eyelets have been used to hold the black layer of paper in place on the background page. The title "Memories" are rub-on letters; the label under the photo is computer type; the poem is a sticker.*

1 Working on a self-healing mat, make a hole for the eyelet with the hole punch tool, using the correct hole setting for the size of the eyelet. (The average size eyelet is 1/8" in diameter; extra large eyelets are 1/4".)

2 Insert the eyelet into the hole from the front.

3 Turn over the paper piece. Place the eyelet setter tip directly on the back side of the eyelet.

4 Using a hammer, tap the back of the setter until the back of the eyelet splits and flattens out.

Setting Eyelets Using an All-in-One Tool

1. Select the appropriate-size hole punch tip and slip into the tool head. Place the paper on the setting mat. Position the tool on the paper where the hole is to be placed.
2. To make the hole, hold the tool vertically and press straight down until you feel a click.
3. Replace the hole punch tip with the correct size eyelet setting tip. Place the eyelet in the hole. Hold the eyelet in place while you turn over the paper.
4. Holding the tool vertically on the eyelet, press straight down on the eyelet until you feel a click. Repeat this step two to three times to completely set the eyelet.

Memories

Mom and Dad-1950

"**LIFE** is not a matter of **milestones**, but of moments."

Rose Fitzgerald Kennedy

Snaps

Snaps, which have solid tops and come in a variety of styles, shapes, and colors, can be used to accent and embellish scrapbook pages. They are attached with a metal setting tool in much the same way that eyelets are attached. You can attach just the front part of the snap so that it is merely decorative. You can also layer papers and set a snap so that it attaches the two pieces together. Or, to make it functional, attach the back part on the background paper, and the front part on the item you wish to snap to the background.

Supplies
- Snap setting tool or all in one tool • Snaps • Paper
- Self-healing cutting mat

1

Place the paper on the setting mat. Position the tool on the paper where the hole is to be placed and make the hole with the hole punch tip.

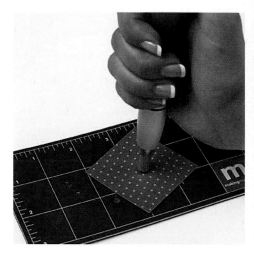

2

Place the snap in the hole and turn over the paper. Use the setting tool to set the snap. This is the backside.

3

This is the front side of the snap.

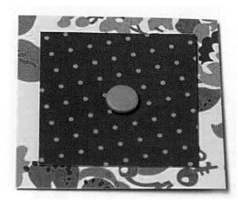

Pictured opposite: *Here the snaps below the photo are merely decorative. All the letters and numbers on the page are stickers. The layer of paper on top of the background paper has been dry brushed with acrylic paint.*

Hinges

Hinges add dimension and decoration to a layout. Hinges can also be functional – use them to attach flaps of paper that can be lifted away to reveal what's underneath.

Hinges are usually attached with brads or snaps. The instructions below show how to attach a hinge with brads; follow the previous instructions for eyelets to attach a hinge with snaps.

Supplies
- Hinge
- Brads
- Needle or paper piercer
- Card stock or heavy paper

1

Position the hinge on the edge of the card stock. Holding paper with one hand, insert the needle completely through the hinge holes.

2

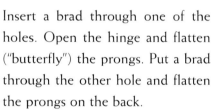

Insert a brad through one of the holes. Open the hinge and flatten ("butterfly") the prongs. Put a brad through the other hole and flatten the prongs on the back.

Pictured on opposite page: At bottom left, a hinge attaches a tag that has been hand torn and sprayed with white spray paint. When the tag is pulled back, there is journaling hidden under it. The top edges of the background paper have also been lightly sprayed with brown transparent spray paint. The edges of the photos have been lightly brushed with opaque paper paint. Rubber stamps decorate the top left and bottom right corners.

ADMIRE

Photo Turns

Photo turns are a great accent for photos or anywhere on a layout that needs just a little something extra. They are attached with a brad or a snap.

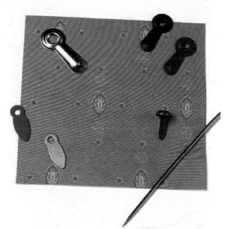

1

Position photo turn on paper.

2

Use a needle or paper piercer to poke a hole through the hole of the photo turn and all the way through the paper.

Supplies
- Photo turns
- Paper or card stock
- Brads or snaps
- Needle or paper piercer

3

Insert a brad through the hole from the front of the paper. Flatten (butterfly) the prongs of the brad.

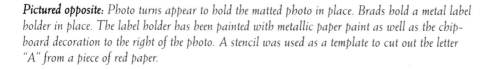

Pictured opposite: *Photo turns appear to hold the matted photo in place. Brads hold a metal label holder in place. The label holder has been painted with metallic paper paint as well as the chipboard decoration to the right of the photo. A stencil was used as a template to cut out the letter "A" from a piece of red paper.*

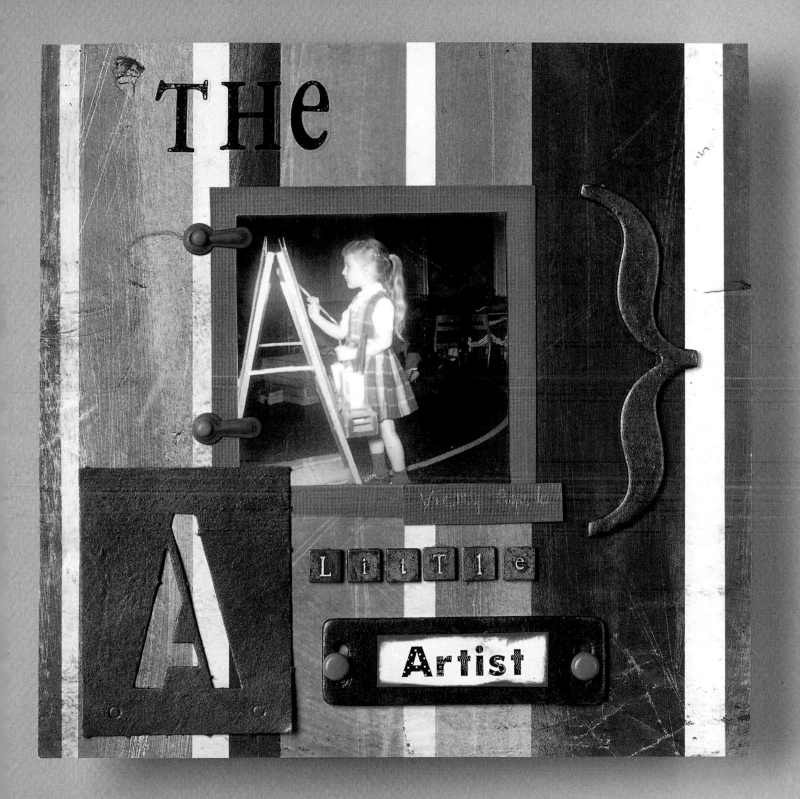

Miscellaneous Accents

Accents such as silk flower petals, clips, charms, and safety pins are easy to attach and make great additions to a layout.

Supplies
- Card stock cutout
- Clip
- Ribbon
- Liquid paper glue

Pictured opposite: A small metal frame with ribbon strip is used to frame the title "Love." The title is a sticker. The dark mat under the photo is torn with a ruler as well as the vertical light paper strip border on left. The designs on the dark border at left edge of paper were done with a punch.

Using a Clip to Hold a Ribbon

1

2

Determine the position of the ribbon and the clip on the paper. Apply glue where the ribbon will be placed.

Place ribbon and press on glue. Place clip on edge of paper over ribbon.

Mom · Cindy · Vicky

LOVE

AGING & TEXTURING TECHNIQUES

Many different looks from one paper can be achieved with aging and texturing techniques – sanding, crumpling, tearing, inking, and bleaching are some of the ways paper can take on a whole new look. Use them to create the distressed look of wear and age, a vintage appearance, or to add unusual textures that will make the layout special.

Sanding

Gentle sanding instantly ages papers. It's a good idea to experiment first with a small scrap of the paper to see how the sanding will affect it. Papers with a white core yield the most dramatic effects.

Sandpaper sheets, a sanding block or sponge, or even an emery board can be used. Sandpaper comes in fine, medium, and coarse grits. Fine or medium is suitable for this technique.

Sanding can give a distressed look to accents like brads or painted chipboard cutouts.

Sanding Paper

Place paper or card stock on a flat surface and sand, using a circular motion.

Sanding a Brad

Rub sandpaper or an emery board across a brad or other element to remove some of the finish. Be careful – you don't want to completely remove all of the paint or finish.

Supplies
- Sandpaper, sanding sponge, or emery board
- Paper or card stock
- Embellishments or accents

Pictured on opposite page: The edges of the background paper have been sanded on this page. The brads attaching the die cut flowers on the left have been sanded also. The title "smile" was done with stamped letters. The dots on the photo mat were done with a punch. There is journaling on the tag hidden under the photo. The pocket for the tag was created by gluing only the top, left, and bottom edges of the photo mat.

Crumpling

Crumpling gives paper more texture, producing a network of fine lines and a high-and-low profile when the paper is smoothed. For additional interest, apply ink to crumpled paper with a cosmetic sponge to highlight the high spots. Use a dry iron to flatten the paper completely, but use care — some coated papers can be damaged by the heat of the iron.

Supplies
- Paper
- Spray bottle and water
- *Optional:* Iron

1

Lightly mist paper with water.

2

Crumple paper with your hands.

3

Flatten and smooth the paper with your hands. *Option:* If desired, iron the paper to smooth it further.

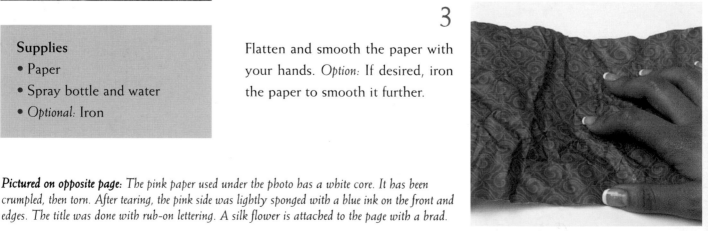

Pictured on opposite page: The pink paper used under the photo has a white core. It has been crumpled, then torn. After tearing, the pink side was lightly sponged with a blue ink on the front and edges. The title was done with rub-on lettering. A silk flower is attached to the page with a brad.

Hand Tearing Paper

One of the easiest scrap-booking techniques is paper tearing. No special tools are required – just your hands.

To make a more controlled tear, use a paint brush with water to paint a line where you want the tear to be. Tear the paper along the line while it is still wet. The paper will tear more easily where it has been wet.

Some papers have a white core. These papers will have a white edge when torn. This edge can be inked, chalked, or used as is.

Pictured on opposite page: The ephemera piece behind the photo is from a child's story book. The page has been hand torn and sprayed with preservative spray. The metal tag at the left of photo has been brushed with metallic rub-on wax and stamped with letters.

1

Hold the paper in your non-dominant hand between your thumb and index finger. With your other (dominant) hand, grasp the paper between your thumb and index finger.

2

Move your dominant hand toward you to tear the paper. Use your thumbs as guides.

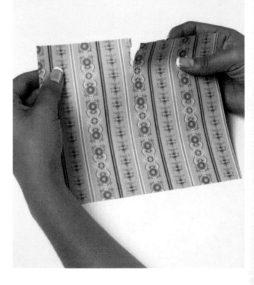

Tearing Paper with a Ruler

You can create a paper with a more uniform torn edge by using a decorative edge ruler. For an easier tear, wet the paper with a cotton swab along the tear line of the ruler. The moisture will weaken the paper slightly. For best results, experiment with a scrap of paper before attempting to tear a large sheet.

1

Place the paper on a flat work surface. Position the ruler on the paper where you want the tear to be.

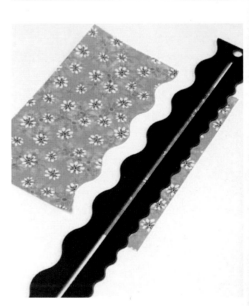

2

Hold the ruler with your dominant hand (right or left), pressing down on the paper firmly. Pull up on the paper with your other hand.

Supplies
- Paper
- Decorative edge metal ruler

Pictured on opposite page: The scallops of the baby's hat is repeated on this page. A scalloped decorative edge ruler was used to tear a green flowered decorative paper strip for the right side of the page. A safety pin punch was used for the decorative element on this strip. This was mounted to the light green background page with glue, then vellum was mounted over it. Another piece of flowered paper was torn with the same ruler for the top layer of paper. The baby photo is in a metal frame with scalloped edges.

I love

Daniel 3 mo.

you

Inking

Use ink to color the edges of scrapbook pages, sponge it over text to highlight words, or rub it on decorative paper to change the color. Apply ink to paper or embellishments after sanding to exaggerate the aged, distressed look.

Ink also can be used to add interest to page elements such as tags, embellishments, and titles. Dye inks of any color work well.

Supplies
- Dye ink pad
- Paper – decorative, card stock, tag
- Cosmetic sponge

1

To ink an element such as a tag, hold the element with one hand and the ink pad with your other hand. Pat the ink pad along the edge of the element.

2

Use a cosmetic sponge to apply the ink to the surface of the paper or element. Load the sponge with ink from the pad and pat or rub the loaded sponge on the paper or element.

Pictured on opposite page: *The edges of the background page and the photo mat have been antiqued with an inkpad. Stickers were used for all the lettering on the page. Under the hinged card at bottom, there is journaling. A photo turn holds the flap in place.*

CONGRATuLatiONS

MOMENTS TO SHARE

sarah

Bleaching Pen

A bleach pen, the kind you buy where laundry detergents are found, is great for bleaching out colored paper. It can be used on the surface of the paper or on the edges. It creates an intriguing aged look.

Pictured on opposite page: *This layout highlights the technique of using bleach to distress a page and add an extra design element. The edges of the mat behind each photo were distressed with a bleach pen. The background paper was purchased as is and has a bleached out look.*

1

Use the point of the pen to draw designs or create faded areas around photos.

2

Use the point to fade out the edges of the paper for an aged look.

3

A bleach pen can create a variety of faded looks. Allow pages to dry thoroughly before proceeding. Drying time can be increased by placing a paper towel onto bleach-edged mat and ironing.

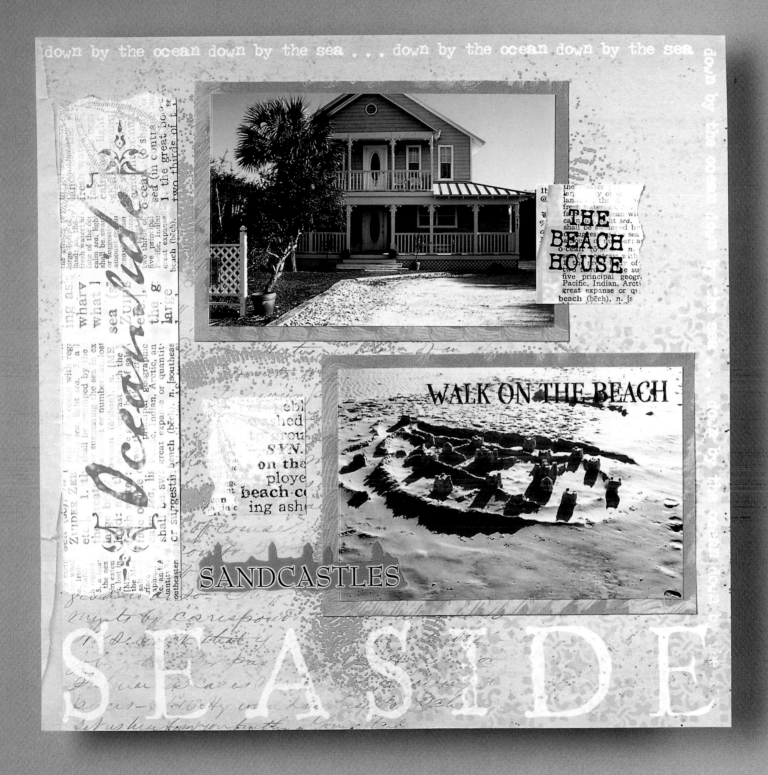

STITCHING

Stitching – either by hand or machine – is a good way to add dimensional elements to scrapbook pages. Stitching can also be used to attach an embellishment such as a pocket or to bind papers together. With hand stitching or embroidery – using cotton floss, silk twist, buttonhole thread, silk ribbon, or thin metallic cord – you can attach embellishments or motifs.

Machine stitching adds decorative detail to any layout; it's also effective for creating borders. Any paper can be machine stitched, even vellum. Basic sewing machines can sew straight and zigzag stitches; more complicated machines come programmed with many decorative stitches.

Machine Stitching

A basic knowledge of the sewing machine is helpful. Practicing on scraps of paper is a good way to learn how your machine will stitch on paper. Be sure to clean the lint from the sewing machine with a brush after each use.

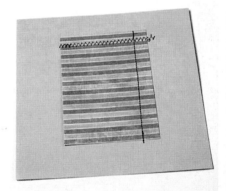

Decorative machine stitching.

1. Select the stitch to be used (zigzag, straight, embroidery). Try it out on a piece of scrap paper.
2. If you're planning to stitch more than one piece, stack the papers to be stitched and place a small piece of tape on the back of one piece so the papers won't shift as you sew.
3. Place the paper(s) under the presser foot. Lower the presser foot and start sewing. Reverse the stitch direction a few times at the beginning and end to anchor the stitches.

Pictured on opposite page: *Various size strips of decorative paper, attached to the background with machine stitching along the edges, give collage a fashion-forward look. Buttons and the use of scalloped decorative edge scissors on the page background complete the look.*

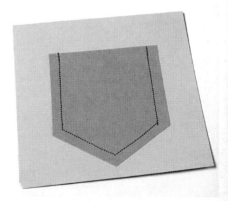

A pocket attached with machine stitching.

We do not remember days, we remember moments.
❋ *Cesare Pavese* ❋

Hand Stitching

Hand stitching is very easy and offers great results. Use hand stitching to embellish pages or to hold elements together. You can use embroidery floss, yarn, or thread – anything that will fit through the eye of a needle. I like to use a template as a stitching guide. You'll have better results if you pierce holes for the stitches before you start to sew with the needle and thread.

Supplies
- Embroidery floss
- Pushpin
- Embroidery needle
- Card stock
- Template
- Pencil with eraser
- Clear tape
- Mouse pad *or* piercing mat

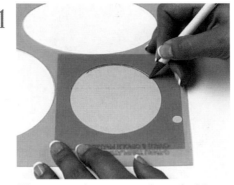

1

Place template on card stock. Use a pencil to trace around the shape.

2

Working on a mouse pad or piercing mat, use a pushpin to punch evenly spaced holes along the traced line. Erase the pencil line.

3

Thread a needle with 18" of embroidery floss. Anchor floss to the back of the card stock with tape. Stitch through the holes created with the pushpin, adding more floss as needed.

4

Anchor the thread end with tape to the back of the card stock.

Pictured on opposite page: *Two flowers have been handstitched above and below the photo. Buttons are glued to the center of the flowers. The flower at the upper left has been stamped then cut out. The center button has been sewn on to attach the flower and the circle layer. Acrylic paint was used to stencil a random design on the mat in back of the photo. The letters spelling "VICKY" are chipboard that has been painted with brown acrylic paint, then sponged with gold acrylic paint. Layers of paper in many sizes and designs give this page a "hip" look.*

Sewing Buttons

With the huge array of designs and colors available, buttons are a good source of decoration and dimension for scrapbook layouts. They can be used as the anchor for a title or at the corners of a mat. Use rows of them as borders or apply them at the centers of petaled flowers. The possibilities are practically endless. You can buy buttons in fabric stores and in the scrapbook aisle of crafts stores, but why not use buttons that hold a memory – a button from a family heirloom or a special garment, for example, or a button associated with a particular photo or time. Yard sales and thrift stores are sources for interesting vintage designs.

There are two basic types of buttons: buttons with holes and buttons with shanks on the back. Buttons with holes can be stitched or glued in place. To use a shank button, remove the shank with a shank cutter or pliers so the back of the button will lay flat against the page and can be glued in place.

Supplies
- Button with holes • Paper
- Paper piercer • Scissors
- Needle • Adhesive dot
- Thread, fiber, or yarn

1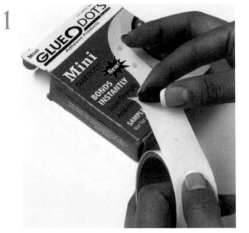

Use an adhesive dot to tack the button to the paper and hold it in place. Place the button on the dot, then peel the dot off the release paper.

2

Place button on paper. Use a paper piercer to poke holes in the paper through the holes in the button.

3

Thread the needle. Sew the button to the paper, running the thread through the pierced holes.

4

Tie thread in a knot to secure. Trim excess. Knots can be tied on the front or back, depending upon the look you want to achieve.

Pictured on opposite page: *The buttons sewn above the title done with a computer are a cute nod to the theme of the page. Decorative edge scissors have been used to cut the mat behind the photo as well as the strip of paper at left. the cut edge of the left strip has been antiqued with an inkpad.*

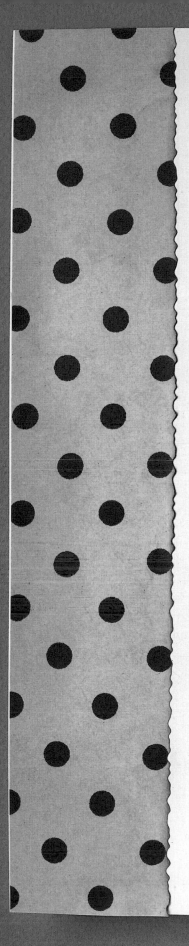

Cute as a Button

Vicky Age 1

DRY EMBOSSING

Dry embossing is a technique that uses a stylus with a blunt, rounded tip and a brass stencil to create a raised image. You work with the stencil underneath the paper and press the paper with the stylus to create a raised image as high as the thickness of the stencil. For dry embossing, you will need a light source, such as a light box or a window, to see the stencil through the paper.

Dry embossing works equally well on card stock, paper, or vellum.

Supplies
- Brass stencil
- Paper
- Stylus
- Light box
- *Optional:* Chalk, cosmetic sponge, sandpaper

Reverse Embossing (Debossing)

A debossed image is simply the reverse side of the embossed image. Follow the same steps as dry embossing, but use the other (recessed) side of the image rather than the raised side.

Pictured on opposite page: Notice the area of the monogram "K." A design was dry embossed on vellum and placed over the sticker monogram. The words "Our Wedding" and "you may kiss the bride" are stickers. The couples name and wedding date is computer journaling. The rounded corners on the photos were done with a corner punch.

1

Turn on the light box. Place the stencil on the light box. Position the paper over the stencil. (If you use a window instead of a light box, tape the brass stencil to the glass and tape the paper in place over the stencil.

2

Use the stylus to trace around the outline of the brass stencil.

3

Lift the paper and turn it over to reveal the raised image.

4

Option: Apply chalk with a cosmetic sponge *or* rub with sandpaper to highlight the embossed image.

you may kiss the bride

Collin and Sarah

December 10, 2006

Our Wedding

K

QUICK EMBELLISHMENTS

Stickers

Fast and easy to apply, self-adhesive stickers provide colors, themes, and design elements to layouts. Available in many colors, shapes, and styles, stickers come in a multitude of finishes.

Stickers come on sheets and rolls, as both individual motifs and border strips. Epoxy stickers are made of raised, dimensional resin and come in clear motifs, words, or letters. Letter stickers are great for titles and captions.

To ensure exact placement, measure with a ruler and mark the placement with a light pencil mark.

Pictured on opposite page: All the lettering on this page is stickers. The photo mats have been cut with decorative edge scissors. The edge of the background paper has been antiqued with an inkpad.

1

Lift the sticker to peel it away from the backing film.

2

Position the sticker and press to adhere to paper.

Chi·ca·go (shə-kä'gō), *n.* 1. a city in northeastern Illinois, on Lake Michigan. 2. famous for the lakefront, Navy Pier, the "L", the Loop, Magnificent Mile, the Sears Tower, museums, Wrigley Field and Marshall Field's.

Chicago

MY kind of TOWN

CHICAGO

Rub-On Transfers

Rub-on transfers are a quick way to add motifs, lettering, or sentiments to scrapbook pages. They serve the same purpose as computer-generated titles and journaling, but they can be placed on surfaces that can't be put through a computer printer and you don't need a computer to use them.

Like stickers, rub-on transfers are available individually, on sheets, or as border strips. Apply a rub-on by placing it face down on paper and rubbing it with a craft stick to transfer the letters or design.

Supplies
- Rub-on transfer
- Paper
- Scissors

1

Use scissors to cut the rub-on transfer from the sheet.

2

Position the rub-on on the paper and rub the design firmly with a craft stick so that the design is "rubbed on" and adhered to the paper.

3

Gently lift the film to reveal the motif.

Pictured on opposite page: The titling is *rub-on lettering. The matted photo is attached to the background page with brads at the four corners.*

Die Cuts

Die cuts are shapes and letters cut from card stock by a machine. (The part of the machine that makes the cut is called the die.) They can be purchased as already-cut cutouts, or you can create them with a personal die cut machine from the paper of your choice. Most scrapbooking stores carry a professional die cut system with a selection of dies. When you purchase paper from the store, using the die cutting system is free.

Die-cut shapes can be adhered with foam dots, liquid glue, adhesive dots, or a glue stick. You can also buy cutouts that were cut with a laser, rather than a die-cutting machine. They are used the same ways as die cuts.

Pictured on opposite page: The flowers on this page are die cuts. They have been attached to the page with sewn-on buttons at their center. Hand stitching adds a decorative element at the left and bottom edges. Resin stickers spell out the two boys' names.

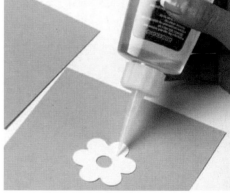

1

Turn over the die cut and apply adhesive to the back.

2

Position the die cut, adhesive side down, on the layout. Press in place.

Tags

Tags add instant dimension to a page. You can buy already-cut plain or decorative tags or trace them with a template on the paper of your choice and cut them out with scissors or a craft knife. You can attach tags with a brad or with any acid-free adhesive. Foam dots are an option if more dimension is desired.

Use tags for titles, journaling, photo mats, and accents. Loop fibers through the hole in the tag for decoration, or glue different papers to a tag for a collage effect. Machine or hand stitch around the tag for a homespun look, or decorate with rubber stamps, paint, or stickers.

Supplies
- Tag
- Paper
- Brad
- Adhesive

1

Turn over the tag. Place a small dab of adhesive on the back.

2

Position the tag, adhesive side down, on paper. Press in place.

3

Make a hole in the paper at the location of the hole in the tag. Insert a brad through the hole and spread the prongs on the back.

Pictured on opposite page: *This page highlights the use of tags to build interest. The tags used include chipboard, card stock, label tag, and decorative paper cut into a circle tag. Card stock or decorative paper tags can be created from paper punches, die cut machines, templates, or purchased already to use. The tags are attached with brads. Purchased decorative dog stickers made it easy to construct the layout.*

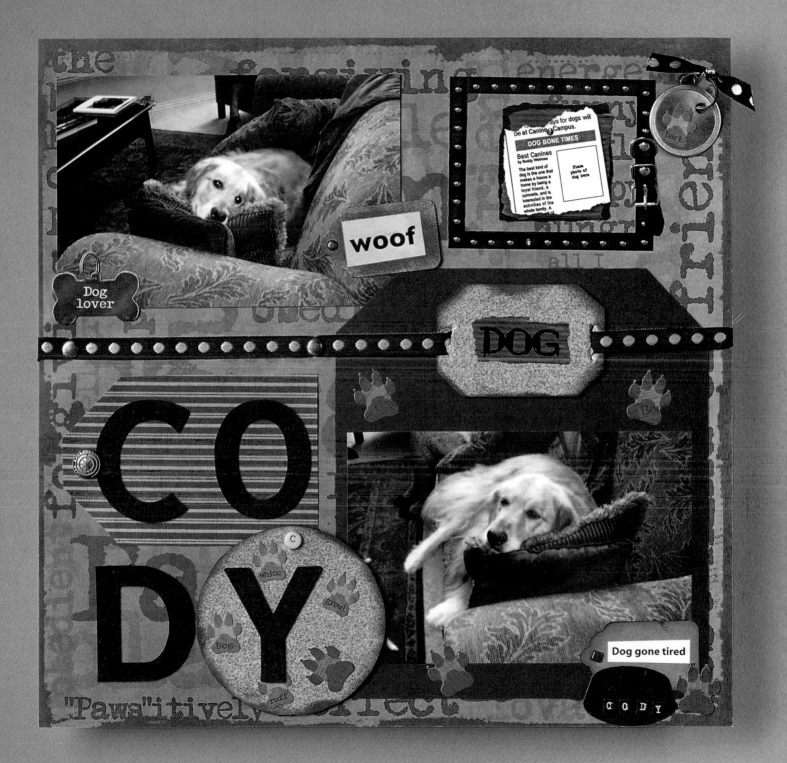

you're the Best!

Pricilla!

I had the pleasure of taking Pricilla Hauser's beginner painting class in 2004. It was an experience I will never forget. The class is held in Florida along a beautiful stretch of beach of the panhandle. She is the best teacher, and is so inspiring. While I learned so much, my painting skills still leave a lot to be desired. I need to find the time to practice! Not only is she a good friend that I adore, but is one of the most talented ladies I know.

STUDIO

Friend

P

art

MEMORIES

Pictured above: *This page is a great example of using tags of all kinds to accent a layout. The small tags were cut from card stock using a paper punch. The large tag was cut from card stock using a template. The medium tags are purchased and decorated with letter stickers. All tags were attached with brads.*

Pictured above: *This tag shape was cut from decorative paper. Snowflakes of every size decorate the page. They were punched out with decorative paper punches, then accented with dimensional metallic paper paint. The title was stamped and embossed on white paper, then each letter was cut out and mounted to page.*

Chipboard Accents

Chipboard is a thick paper product made from recycled paper. It is commonly used as a backing for notepads and business forms. For scrapbooking, chipboard comes in many shapes and letter styles, both plain and printed with designs and is sold in most scrapbooking departments. Versatile and inexpensive, chipboard accents can be painted, inked, covered with paper, sanded, or covered with rub-on transfers. Use chipboard letters to spell out titles or journaling; add cutout motifs anywhere on a page where dimension is desired.

Adhere chipboard accents with liquid glue, adhesive dots, a glue stick, or foam dots. Chipboard tags can be attached with a brad.

Covering a Chipboard Cutout with Paper

Supplies
• Chipboard cutout
• Paper
• Liquid adhesive
• Scissors
• *Optional*: Sentiment or journaling

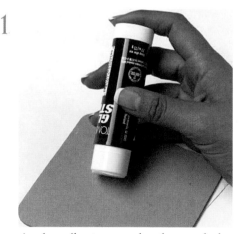

1

Apply adhesive to the front of the chipboard piece.

2

Place paper, right side down, on your work surface. Put the adhesive side of the chipboard piece on the wrong side of the paper. Press the chipboard piece to the paper to ensure secure adhesion.

3

Trim the paper around the edge of the chipboard piece with scissors.

4

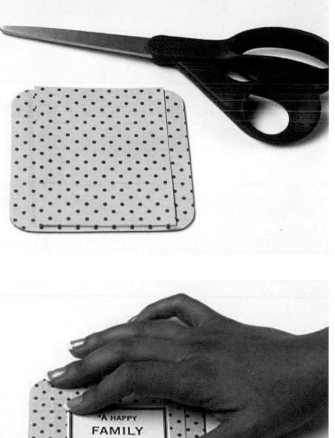

Turn over the piece to reveal the paper-covered surface.

5

Use the paper-covered piece as a frame for a sticker with a sentiment or hand journaling. You could also ink the edges, or add buttons or rubber-stamped images.

"A HAPPY **FAMILY** IS BUT AN EARLIER **HEAVEN.**"
JOHN BOWRING

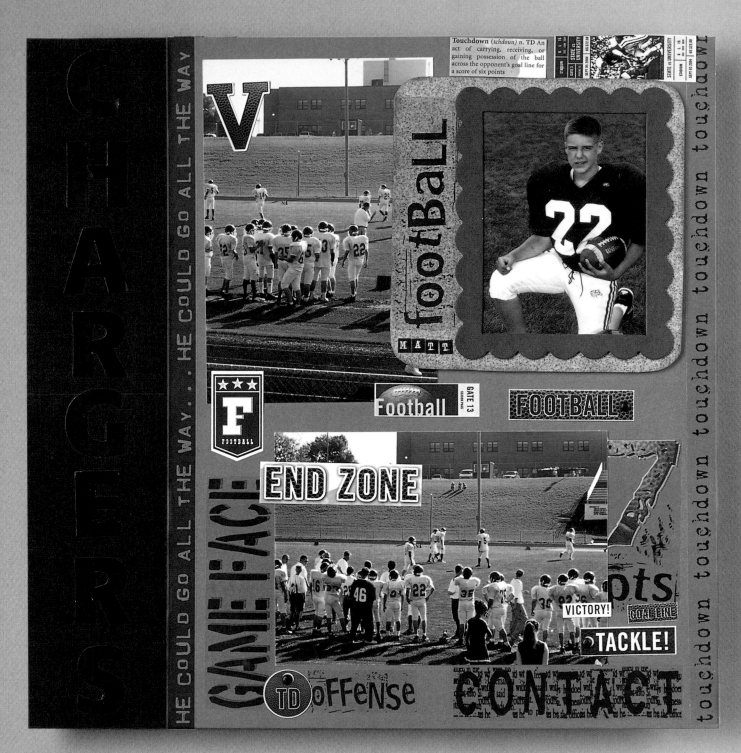

Pictured above: *A chipboard frame was die cut then painted with acrylic paint. It was mounted, along with the photo, onto a paper-covered chipboard square piece. This layout is a great example of how to use themed stickers.*

Pictured above: The page title, "My Sisters" was done with chipboard letters that have been colored with ink. The child's name is spelled out with metal letters and the date is computer lettering.

Transparencies

Transparencies – the thin see-through plastic sheets originally used with overhead projectors – can be used on layouts as overlays for adding journaling. Use them to cover entire pages, a photo, or individual page elements as an accent.

You can print on transparencies with a computer printer or write on them with markers and place the text anywhere on the page. To accent transparencies, frame them with metal frames or slide mounts.

Supplies

- Transparency with journaling (Buy the type of transparency intended for computer printing and print the words on your home computer.)
- Matted photo
- 4 brads
- Hole punch

1

Position the printed transparency on the matted photo. Trim the transparency even with the edges of the mat.

2

Use a hole punch to make a hole through all the layers in each corner. Install a brad through the hole in each corner to attach the transparency to the matted photo.

Pictured on opposite page: *All the lettering except the date and the "memories" journaling is a transparency that is attached to the page with brads. The edges of the background paper have been antiqued with ink.*

song of the

Sea

end at the
shore or
the hearts
of those who
listen to it

— Kahlil Gibran

2006

[mem·or·ies]
that which is created as present becomes past

Oceanside

seaside beachside oceanside

Slide Mounts

Slide mounts are great for adding a little dimension and can serve as frames for photos and small blocks of text. Some come already decorated with paper or a design. You can also customize slide mounts with stamps, paint, ink, or stickers.

Supplies
- Slide mount
- Glue stick
- Scissors
- Item to be framed

1

Use a photo or type a title, saying, or caption on the computer and print on paper. Place behind the slide mount.

2

Trim the paper even with the edges of the slide mount.

3

Rub a glue stick on the back of the slide mount. Press the front side of the paper in place over the glue. Attach slide mount to page.

Pictured on opposite page: The slide mount was purchased with printing on it. It frames the date that was done with stickers. The title "Prom" is also sticker letters. The other designs on the page are rub-ons.

PROM

2006

memories

Pictured above: S is for Sarah. This layout highlights the use of a purchased decorated slide mount to frame one of the letters. The frame was adhered with dispenser tape.

Pictured on opposite page: On this 8-1/2" x 11" page, a large size slide mount frames just part of the photo. The decorated slide mount was purchased as is and adhered to the page with paper glue. Other embellishments include photo turns and a tag that is decorated with machine stitching and rick-rack.

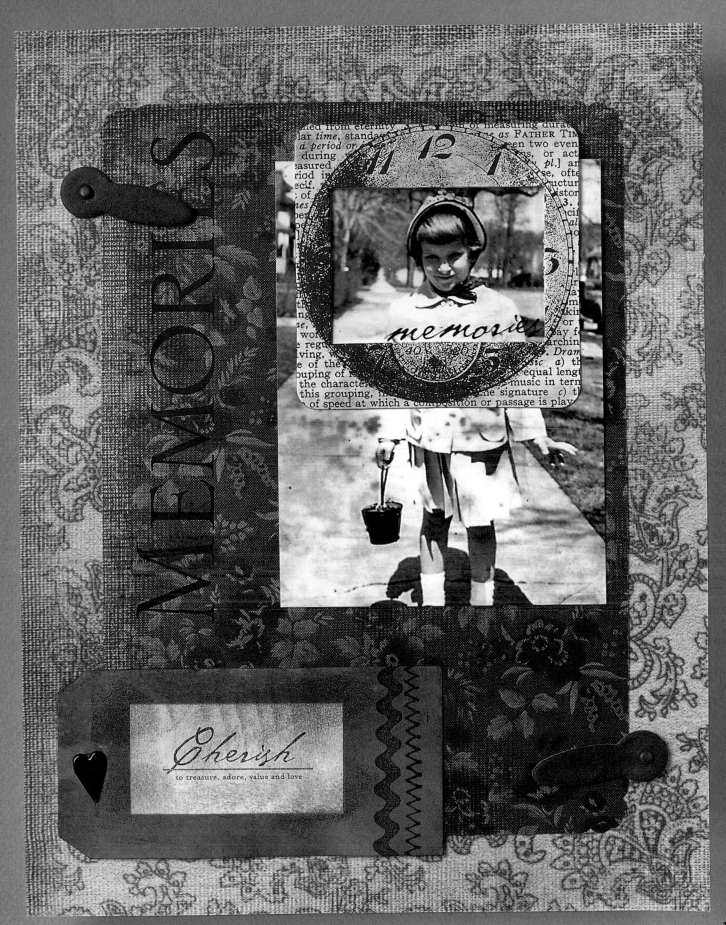

CREATING POCKETS

Pockets are a great way to conceal journaling or hold a keepsake from a memorable event. You can buy ready-to-use pockets, or make your own — pockets are easy to make. Pockets can be any shape, including squares, rectangles, trapezoids, or the familiar tapered shape with a pointed bottom like the back pockets of blue jeans. You can also glue an envelope to a scrapbook page and use it as a pocket.

Attach pockets with any adhesive or with fasteners such as brads or eyelets. Decorate pockets with stickers or embellishments for added interest.

Supplies
- Paper or card stock, cut to the size and shape desired
- Adhesive (your choice)
- Scissors
- Tag with journaling

1

Turn over the pocket so the back side is facing up. Apply adhesive to the edges of three sides.

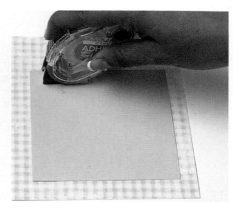

2

Press the pocket, adhesive side down, on the layout.

3

Slide a tag with journaling (or other item) in the pocket.

Pictured on opposite page: The pocket on this page was made by layering a strip of polka dot paper at the top edge of a piece of red paper. The label on the pocket is a sticker. The bottom and sides were glued down so that a tag with hand journaling could be slipped into the top of the pocket. Machine stitching attaches the striped paper layer to the background paper.

CARE·FREE
1. without a care
in the world
2. happy, blissful
existence
3. no troubles

THE
BOYS

THIS PHOTO WAS

LITTLE BOYS
1. curious 2. mischievous
3. energetic 4. fear nothing
5. future fathers

Pictured above: *A purchased library style pocket was glued to the scrapbook page. The pocket holds the invitation to the party as a memento. The pocket is trimmed with sticker candles and glued on rick-rack.*

Pictured above: *Just You and Me. This layout highlights the use of a pocket to hide a tag with journaling. A sewing machine was used to sew the pocket in place, leaving the top open. A sewing machine is a great alternative to glue or tape to join papers or decorative accents to a scrapbook page. The title is cut out letters that are glued to a chipboard piece that has an antiqued edge done with ink.*

Pictured above: Graduation Day. This layout highlights the use of ephemera to decorate the page. The diploma was copied and printed onto vellum as well as the program copied onto a gray paper to coordinate with the background paper. The vellum was attached with brads. Coordinating graduation stickers were used as accents.

Pictured above: Memories of Paris. The old postcards are the highlight of this page. Stickers such as the ones used for the title and journaling can be purchased at most scrapbook departments.

METRIC CONVERSION CHART

Inches to Millimeters and Centimeters

Inches	MM	CM	Inches	MM	CM
1/8	3	.3	2	51	5.1
1/4	6	.6	3	76	7.6
3/8	10	1.0	4	102	10.2
1/2	13	1.3	5	127	12.7
5/8	16	1.6	6	152	15.2
3/4	19	1.9	7	178	17.8
7/8	22	2.2	8	203	20.3
1	25	2.5	9	229	22.9
1-1/4	32	3.2	10	254	25.4
1-1/2	38	3.8	11	279	27.9
1-3/4	44	4.4	12	305	30.5

Yards to Meters

Yards	Meters	Yards	Meters
1/8	.11	3	2.74
1/4	.23	4	3.66
3/8	.34	5	4.57
1/2	.46	6	5.49
5/8	.57	7	6.40
3/4	.69	8	7.32
7/8	.80	9	8.23
1	.91	10	9.14
2	1.83		

INDEX

Continued on next page

INDEX